Prayer
is the
Answer

TITLES BY JOSEPH MURPHY

AVAILABLE IN PRINT AND EBOOK FROM G&D MEDIA

This Is It

How to Use Your Healing Power

Living Without Strain

Love is Freedom

Magic of Faith

Peace Within Yourself

Pray Your Way Through It

Prayer is the Answer

Quiet Moments with God

Techniques in Prayer Therapy

The Miracles of Your Mind

Traveling with God

You Can Change Your Whole Life

AVAILABLE IN EBOOK FROM G&D MEDIA

Believe in Yourself

Fear Not

How to Attract Money

How to Use the Power of Prayer

Nuclear Religion

Riches Are Your Right

Stay Young Forever

The Healing Power of Love

The Meaning of Reincarnation

Why Did This Happen to Me?

Prayer is the Answer

The Meaning of the Sacraments

Joseph Murphy

Ph.D., D.D.

Published 2019 by Gildan Media LLC
aka G&D Media
www.GandDmedia.com

Design by Meghan Day Healey of Story Horse, LLC

Library of Congress Cataloging-in-Publication Data is available upon request

ISBN: 978-1-7225-0136-5

10   9   8   7   6   5   4   3   2   1

Contents

1

The Healing Power of God and How to Use It

Baptism and Original Sin Explained

The word *sacrament* means a binding compact within the sanctuary of the soul. In simple language it is the harmonious relationship between the conscious and subconscious mind bringing you harmony, health, and peace. The word *sacrament* comes from the Latin word *sacrare* which means to make sacred, to make holy.

This book deals with the inner or real psychological meaning of the sacrament revealing a magnificent process of spiritual rebirth. As you peruse, meditate on, and apply the simple techniques outlined herein, you will discover a power within you which can lift you out of a sickbed, making you whole, radiant, and perfect. Here you will find the key to happiness and peace of mind.

The greatest prison in the world is the prison of the mind. Decide to be free now and to shape your life along Godlike ways. In every page you will learn about and how to use a wonderful, magical, healing power which will bind up the wounds of the broken-hearted, which will proclaim liberty to the captives, and the opening of the prison to those who are bound by fear, failure, misery, and pain.

Solve that problem now. Decide to be prosperous. Smooth out all difficulties. Move onward and upward through the Power of God within you.

In order to advance spiritually, we must give up the lesser for the greater; this is symbolized in the Bible by the sacrifice of animals. What the latter really means is to give up negative, destructive thinking, all negative emotions, and to make a place in the soul (subconscious mind) for the higher qualities of goodness, love, and truth. In other words the sacrifice of animals meant the practice of the great law of substitution, such as giving love for hatred, bringing joy where there is sadness, bringing light where there is darkness, and entering into the spirit of forgiveness where ill will is. The slaughtering of beasts mentioned in the Bible is not slaughtering in the ordinary sense of the word. It is true, of course, that people in various parts of the world, not understanding the laws of the mind and the ways of God, propitiated their gods. There are parts of the world where they still offer up human sacrifices. In my recent round-the-world lecture tour I heard of many instances from governmental officials and other prominent people.

In ancient times when famine came, crops were destroyed, or cattle died from epidemic, men offered up bullocks and cattle. All this disaster, they believed, was inflicted by an angry God. In order to appease this angry Being, they offered him their gory sacrifices in the belief that thus they would gain his good will. The idea behind this was to give up something near and dear to them in order to achieve their objective or goal. This age-old, jungle superstition prevails to this day; the British Government has made heroic efforts to stamp it out in all parts of the Empire. Primitive man has offered up his own children—sons and daughters—to propitiate his gods.

I observed a man in India whose arms were paralyzed, and who was blind as a result of staring at the sun. He brought the paralysis and the blindness on himself voluntarily because he wanted to atone for his sins, thinking that by torturing himself he was pleasing his god. I have seen others who have crippled, distorted, and twisted themselves into all sorts of weird forms, miserable husks of what once were men. All this has been done to appease their gods or atone for their sins.

I heard a man in South Africa say, "I will give up drinking and cursing if God will spare my boy." Here again is a phase of the old racial belief—dread of an angry God. All these procedures and practices are due to the fact that man has postulated a god apart, an inscrutable, tyrannical, oriental, despotic sultan ruling in the skies. His concept seems to be that God is some sort of a cannibalistic Moloch living in the skies who has to be appeased by blood-letting sacrifices and suffering.

Last July I visited a sacred shrine in the Orient. I chatted with a young girl at the shrine who had traveled four hundred miles to visit this Buddhistic shrine. She had not eaten for three days. She lit many candles and brought lots of fruit as an offering to Buddha. She prayed for a long time each day and each day offered up more candles and fruit. She said to me she was sure that if she fasted and spent all she could on gifts to Buddha, her prayers would be answered. I noticed she emptied her purse before the shrine of Buddha. Her prayer was answered not because she lit candles or gave oranges and rice to Buddha, but because of her belief. According to her belief was it done unto her. All her sacrifices were of no avail and meant nothing insofar as the laws of mind are concerned, for the law of life is the law of belief.

If man will sit still, relax his mind and body, and believe that his prayer is answered—it will be answered. Candles, oranges, journeys, and pilgrimages are not necessary. It would be silly to say that such practices at shrines are bad; they are not. These people believe that God looks with favor on their practices, and in that way they experience a feeling of inward *grace* following their ritual, ceremony, or offering. However, all such observances are really based on ignorance and lack of understanding.

"To what purpose is the multitude of your sacrifices to me, saith the Lord. I am full of the burnt offering of rams and the fat of beasts and I delight not in the blood of bullocks or of lambs and he goats." Isaiah 1:11. The meaning of the above quotation is this: Any state of mind other than complete mental acceptance of your desire or ideal is an abomination unto the Lord. All sacrifices are superstitions and mean nothing. All that is necessary is to feel the reality of your prayer; live, move, and act in that mental atmosphere, as though it were already a fact. With that fixed attitude of mind, your belief will objectify itself. This is the meaning of "Believe that you have received and you shall receive."

In this book we are going to remove all the wrappings and the trappings, and to reveal the principle at work and how to operate it scientifically.

To think that God requires you to shed your blood for someone, or sit in an ant heap until your feet are eaten up, as some men do in India is a monstrous absurdity and makes a cannibal of God instead of a God of love.

A man in London said to me last year, "We are here to suffer because the Bible says 'We glory in tribulation.'" ROMANS 5:3. Here is another instance of a man thinking that his redemption could only come through suffering. I explained this paragraph. When you find yourself in tribulation; i.e., if you have a problem, you seek the answer, the solution, the way out— that is to glory in your tribulation. The word *glory* comes from two words, *glow* and *ray*. Ray. means the Light of God or the Infinite Intelligence which knows only the answer; and the glow means the warmth, joy, the thrill you feel when you know that the action of God is now taking place where the problem is; as you remain faithful to this fixed attitude, the dawn comes and the shadows flee away.

Be sure you glory in your tribulation the next time. It is a simple technique of prayer. We must not twist it or distort it, placing more chains on people already suffering enough. Look upon the Bible as a story about yourself—a parable—a tale always to be told. The Bible is a great psychological document teaching you how to release the Power, the Wisdom, and the Intelligence of God lodged in your unconscious depths. You can begin to make a sacrifice now. I assure you, it will be the turning point of your life. Give up all beliefs in other powers, simply enthrone in your mind One Spiritual Power and give allegiance to that One Power only. Recognizing only One Power, uniting with It, knowing that its Life, Love, Truth, and Beauty are forever being expressed through you is the real sacrifice—all else is superstition and rank nonsense.

Here is how to practice the sacrifice. A friend of mine was involved in a lawsuit recently. The other man was lying and had sworn falsely. My friend was highly incensed, hostile, and full of recriminations. I explained to him that he would have to sacrifice his negative feelings by supplanting them with the mood of love and faith in the Absolute Principle of Harmony. Instead, therefore, of wasting his energy and vitality by indulging in negative thoughts toward the man who was suing him, he took his mind off him altogether and began to pray in this manner: "The absolute Harmony of God reigns supreme in the minds and hearts of all involved in this legal case and there is a divine, harmonious solution. Divine Justice and Divine Love prevail." He repeated that statement of Truth knowingly, feelingly, and meaningfully until he felt it registered in his deeper mind. You inscribe these Truths in the heart by repetition, faith, and expectancy. He imagined these truths sinking into his deeper mind like seeds being deposited in the soil. After a few days he was at peace about the whole matter and subsequent events verified and testified to his inner mental attitude of poise and confidence. A verdict was rendered in his favor which blessed all. It was Divine Order. "Order is Heaven's first law." (Troward).

The above incident explains the whole idea of sacrifice and sacraments. The man gave up the mood of a problem and entered into the sense of oneness with God and His Law of Absolute Harmony. He freed himself from fear and worry and gave himself faith and confidence. We said a sacrament means to make sacred or holy. The word *holy* means to be integrated, to be at peace, to be healed, to be poised, serene, and calm. You are holy when your mind is at peace, when you are healthy, happy, and full of good will to all. There are various degrees of wholeness and perfection. You offer up a sacrifice when you turn away from pain and dwell on God's River of Peace flooding your mind and body. You have given up the burden of pain and decided to enjoy relaxation and perfect health.

A ship in distress on the high seas ofttimes lightens its cargo by casting overboard surplus freight in order to enable the ship to speed its way to a port of safety. Every time you pray, you are partaking of one of the sacraments and sacrificing something, because when you pray, you turn away from and give up a limitation of some kind.

For example, give up the idea of poverty and feast on the idea of plenty. Give up the idea of hate and feast on the idea of love. Give up the idea of sorrow and feast on the idea of peace. Give up the idea of envy and feast on the idea of good will. Praying in this manner you are really sacrificing because you are giving up the lesser for the greater. Philo Judaeus of Alexandria summed it all up in a few words when he said that the only thing you can offer God is "Praise and Thanksgiving." How beautiful, soul-stirring, and yet how true!

The Truth student is offering himself daily on a cross and shedding his blood in this sense. The cross means you are crossing over from darkness to light, from ignorance to understanding, from fear to faith, from pain to health, from ill will to good will. The Truth student is always psychologically crossing over; i.e., he rises with his two wings of thought and feeling above the barrier, the handicap, or the problem, and rests in the Secret Place, the inner recesses of his mind, where he contemplates the Divine solution. There he imagines and pictures the solution, the way things ought to be; he sheds his blood. Blood is life, which means he pours life, love, and feeling into the picture and makes it real. In other words, he makes his prayer alive. He senses and feels the reality of the invisible idea. The idea is real; therefore, he rejoices in the idea and gives thanks for the idea. In this way the student dies to the belief in the problem and rises to the belief in the answer, feeling in his heart that his prayer is answered. He has entered into the joy of the answered prayer; he has shed his blood for the other and saved him from his problem.

You will now see how simple it is to perceive the truth of the Bible. Let me illustrate. A friend of mine in Sydney, Australia, dined with me in the Australia Hotel, Australia's loveliest hotel. He told me he had a tumor. He was a very fine Truth student and had a class for some Protestant clergymen twice weekly where he taught them the inner meaning of the Bible. We decided to pray about it. Impulsively I said to him, "I will shed my blood for you on the cross."

He replied, "You know, that is the perfect way to pray." I was delighted to hear him say that and asked him to elaborate. He told me that in an esoteric school in India where he had studied, the Yogi always had said of prayer that the passover and crucifixion stories express the perfect way of prayer. (See my book *Peace within Yourself.*)

I stayed eight days in Sydney, and again stopped there en route from New Zealand to India. I prayed for him night and morning. In this way I made his request my own, saying to myself, "I have to cleanse my own mind of the belief of a tumor." The cross I carried was his desire for health which now became my concept of health and perfection. I knew, in order for crucifixion to take place, the idea of his perfect health, harmony, and perfection would have to pass from my conscious mind to my subconscious mind; i.e., the idea would pass over from the conscious mind and become a fixed impression or belief in the subconscious mind.

Crucifixion means crossing over from the conscious to the subconscious mind. When you succeed in impressing your subconscious mind with the belief in perfect health—healing follows. You become fixed in the belief (crucifixion) that it is so.

Every night and morning I prayed this way:

"John Jones, my friend, is God's man. He is pure spirit. God's wholeness, purity, and perfection are made manifest and reflected in every atom of his being. This idea of harmony, perfect health, and peace is now impressed in my mind, and I know he is made whole, pure, and perfect. God and His Love are being fully expressed in his mind and body." I quietly affirmed this every night and morning after entering into a drowsy, sleepy, meditative state. I shed blood for him, figuratively speaking, meaning I gave life to the words. *Blood* means life. I felt them as true. The word in the Bible means feeling, awareness, conviction. It is a mood, tone, an inner, fixed mental attitude. I had to die psychologically to the belief in a tumor and resurrect the idea of his perfect health and harmony. He prayed in a similar manner for himself. There was a complete healing in his case.

Anyone with ordinary common sense, a high school education, and an open mind will see at once the whole meaning of being saved by the blood of the lamb and all such kindred statements. The *lamb* means God, Life, the Healing Principle; the *blood of the lamb* means the Life, Power, Wisdom, and Intelligence of God in action. Could anything be more simple? If lost in the jungle, the Intelligence of God would lead you out if you turned within, and said, "God is guiding me now and reveals to me the perfect path." The way would be shown you, and you would be governed by an Over-Shadowing Presence and compelled to move in the right direction toward your freedom. You were saved by the blood of the lamb. Do you hear? Can you see? Is it plain? Could it be simpler? You offer yourself up to God when you dedicate all your thoughts and feelings to God. Feeling follows thought. When all your thoughts are God's thoughts, God's Power is with your thoughts of good.

I said to the students attending the lectures on the "Inner Meaning of the Sacraments" that they would hear very familiar words, but that I wanted them to hear the words spoken in an unfamiliar way. Let us take, for example, the following admonition given by Moses to the children of Israel, "Never leave any vessel uncovered." The *vessel* is your mind which you are supposed to guard, watch, supervise, and govern so that all sorts of sundry concepts of a negative nature cannot penetrate. In other words you should be busy filling your mind with God's ideas and verities so that there will be no room in your mind for negative and destructive thoughts. If you met someone on the street and he invited you to the slums, you would in all probability say, "No," offering as an excuse, "There are gangsters, assassins, and murders in those places, and I don't wish to go." You go down the slums of your mind when you indulge in the emotion of resentment, jealousy, and ill will. These gangsters who dwell in the slums of your mind will rob you of vitality, peace, happiness, health, and joy, and leave you a physical and mental wreck. Walk the sunlit streets of your mind and associate with wonderful companions, such as goodness, truth, and beauty. These companions will lead you into ways of pleasantness and paths of peace.

Your conscious mind must, therefore, act as a cover for the subconscious so that false beliefs, errors, fears, etc., floating about cannot enter your deeper mind and pollute it. The cover is your conscious, choosing, volitional, active mind. Watch carefully what thoughts, concepts, and ideas you choose to think upon. All our diseases are created by our own mind. Our mind is creative. If we think good, good follows; if we think evil, evil will follow. If you had free will, which you say you have, would you choose illness, lack, limitation, etc? Don't surrender your spiritual dominion.

Does your free will consist in making the wrong choice—a belief and faith in outer effects, in external causes? When you awaken to your inner power, you will choose only from God's storehouse. You will decide to select whatever things are true, lovely, and of good report. Your choice will always be some great Truth of God to meditate on. You will choose the positive, the ideal, the goal, the solution, the way out.

The teaching of the sacraments is to get you back to the real free choice of good. How can you call yourself a free man with free will if you are held in chains to the belief in sin, sickness, hate, and are kept there by wrong instruction?

Before discussing the subject of Baptism, let us explain *original sin*. These two words are symbolic of the negative state of ignorance, a blindness to things spiritual. In the *Dictionary of Sacred Languages*, original sin represents a fall or descent into matter, in other words God becoming man. There is only One Being. Whenever a child is born, it is the One Being dramatizing himself as that child. When the child is born, whether the King of England or the man in the slums, it is born into all that its environment represents. It is born into the race belief, subject to the mental atmosphere of the home, and all those who come in contact with it.

Quimby said that a child was like a white tablet on which anyone who came along could write something. The dominant mental atmosphere of the parents during the creative act determines the type child that comes forth. (See my book on reincarnation which explains why abnormal children are born). All that original sin means when stated in simple, everyday language is a sense of separation from God. The child is at the mercy of the parents and grows up in the image and likeness of the mental and emotional states of the home. The Wisdom, Power, and Intelligence of God are resident in the child because the Kingdom of God is within all of us, and God is the very life of us.

The false beliefs, fears, and opinions of parents are impressed on the subconscious mind of the child, and he becomes conditioned accordingly; this is the stain of original sin or the immersion of all men in the race mind. The *sacrament of baptism* symbolically represents man awakening to his inner powers, discovering for example, that the Wisdom, Intelligence, and Love of God are within him, awaiting his use. When we discover the creative power of our thought, and realize that thought and feeling create our destiny, we move out of the race mind or law of averages, as it is called by Troward, and mold, fashion, and shape our own destiny.

Man, unaware of his spiritual power, makes all kinds of errors and wrong choices. When he begins to think on whatsoever things are true, beautiful, noble, exalted, and Godlike, he finds that the creative mind responds accordingly, and that happiness and peace result; this procedure is called wisdom by Quimby or the way of health and happiness. If your thoughts are wise, your actions will be wise. Action and reaction are found everywhere. Using the knowledge of the interaction of the conscious and subconscious mind and seeing that the relationship is harmonious and peaceful, the individual performs the true function and meaning of the sacrament.

The conscious mind is the analytical, natural, reasoning mind. It has the capacity to choose. It is personal and selective. The subconscious mind is impersonal and non-selective, and reasons deductively only. It is somewhat like the soil. Whatever you think and feel as true, the subconscious will accept and bring forth as a condition, experience, and event. The subconscious does not argue with you; it merely accepts the premise of your conscious mind, whether true or false, and proceeds to bring it to a logical, sequential conclusion.

This power of the subconscious acceptance is the reason why it is extremely important to choose wisely and select your ideas, thoughts, and plans based on the Golden Rule and the Law of Love. Never admit anything to your conscious mind which will not bless, heal, and inspire you. Ask yourself, "Is this thought or idea good? Will it lift me up? Is it Godlike? Where does it come from? Will it bless the other person"? If your thought, idea, plan, or purpose does not meet these general spiritual specifications, discard it as unfit for the house of God. You are really coming out of the race mind and entering into what Troward calls the Fifth Kingdom when you recognize the spiritual power within you as Almighty, One, and Indivisible. Looking upon It as the only cause and power, knowing at the same time that it is responsive to your through, you have discovered God, the Creative Power. Now you are a citizen of the Fifth Kingdom and no longer subject to race mind. You are now removing the stain of original sin because you reject the false beliefs, opinions, and traditions of man. You give no power whatever to the created world, realizing it is an effect, not a cause. Your allegiance is to the spiritual power within. You love it and you are devoted to it. Let the following be your daily prayer: "I am a channel through which God's Love, Beauty, Harmony, Peace, Opulence, and Intelligence flow. All the qualities, attributes, and potencies of God are now being expressed through me in a wonderful way. It is wonderful."

As you claim this several times a day, and as you feel its truth written in your heart and inscribed in your inward parts, your world will magically melt into the image and likeness of your habitual thinking.

Baptism is a symbol of purification of the subconscious mind by Truth or right thinking. Dr. Nicoll states that the object of all sacred writings is to convey higher meaning and higher knowledge in terms of ordinary knowledge as a starting point. To understand the sacraments you must see them psychologically and perceive another level of meaning. The whole purpose and intention of the sacraments is to bring about an inner change, a transformation of the mind and heart so that man experiences a spiritual rebirth. The stories in the Bible are to be interpreted psychologically; otherwise, they become full of contradictions and absurdities.

Rebirth means to ascend to a higher level of understanding or spiritual awareness. In baptism you can see the priest or minister pouring water over the head of the one to be baptized. You can hear the words, "I baptize thee in the name of the Father, the Son, and of the Holy Ghost." To say that man can be awakened spiritually or experience an inner transformation or rebirth by jumping into a pool of water or by having water poured on him is sheer nonsense. What is the meaning of water? The Bible uses outer, concrete tangible things to represent inner mental attitudes, feelings, and beliefs.

Let us take a few examples of what water means. "Whosoever drinketh of this water shall thirst again: But whosoever drinketh of the water that I shall give him shall never thirst; but the water that I shall give him shall be in him a well of water springing up into everlasting life." John 4:13–14. Here Jesus is referring to spiritual refreshment—divine inspiration. It means divine guidance or the ray of light which comes into a darkened, confused mind.

Quiet your mind, get still, say to yourself, "God has the answer." Know it, believe it, and the moment you least expect, the response, the idea, or answer will come suddenly into your conscious mind like toast pops out of a toaster; this is the well of water within your depths which wells up and refreshes the arid areas of your mind secreting the perfume of God's Healing Essence. I can't imagine anyone conceiving water here as meaning actual physical water. In ancient times and in all sacred languages, *water* was a symbol for Truth or the Eternal Reality and source of all manifestations. Water denotes unity, oneness, wholeness, purity, motion, or absence of parts. God is One and Indivisible.

"Infinity," as Troward says, "cannot be divided or multiplied." There are no divisions or quarrels in it. There cannot be two powers as one would neutralize and cancel out the other. Believing in One Power whose wholeness, purity, and perfection are flowing through you causes you to move mentally in a sense of oneness with all things good. You begin to reproduce all the qualities of God through self-contemplation of the spirit. You are then truly baptized because you are letting God's Truth anoint your intellect. Furthermore, your thoughts, words, and actions conform to spiritual standards and the Law of Unity which is the bond of peace.

Water is used also in the Bible for knowledge. "The words of a man's mouth are as deep waters, and the wellspring of wisdom as a flowing brook." PROVERBS 18:4. A beautiful way to pray is to shut the door of the senses, go asleep to the world, and become alive to the Power of God within.

For example, if you wish to sell your home now as you read these pages begin to imagine the broker or a loved one congratulating you on the sale of the home. Feel the joy and thrill of the fact it is sold. (Believe ye have it now and ye shall receive.) Rejoice in that idea. Give thanks that it is sold. Enter into the reality of the state sought. Your feeling is the spirit of God moving over the water—your mind. Your mind is the water, or you could say your feeling is the water. It really doesn't matter. The fact is water takes the shape of any vessel into which it is poured; likewise your creative mind brings to pass whatever you feel as true. Your fixed states of mind become conditions, events, and experiences.

One of the meanings of water is mind. Your mind is forever moving or flowing like water, psychologically speaking. As you read this your mind is moving and traveling psychologically from idea to idea, from thought to thought. When you contemplate the Divine solution, the perfect answer, when you realize that God solves all problems, and when you trust the Absolute Law of Harmony and Perfection to prevail, you can pray like the Psalmist (PSALMS 46:4) who said, "There is a river, the streams whereof shall make glad the city of God." The *city* of God is your mind at peace, and the *streams* are the Godlike thoughts entertained by you. When you are thirsty, water refreshes you; likewise when you are perplexed, confused, and agitated, water, or spiritual knowledge, will refresh and restore your mind to peace. "And whosoever shall give to drink unto one of these little ones a cup of cold water only in the name of a disciple, verily I say unto you, he shall in no wise lose his reward." MATTHEW 10:42.

It would be foolish to read this inspired passage and think it refers to a cup of cold water. In all probability you would heat the water before giving it to the child. The word *cup* means the heart or subconscious mind. Notice the shape of the cup it can receive; likewise, your mind must be open and receptive before you can receive the Truth. Your mind (cup) must be like a parachute. A parachute is no good except it opens up. You can give yourself a cup of cold water as you read these pages and apply the simple truths elaborated on. You may also pass on these ideas to others thereby giving the little ones a cup of water. The *little ones* refer to all of us who have, at best, only a little knowledge of God and the way He works. No one can ever encompass and comprehend Infinity; i.e., the finite mind cannot understand the Infinite, *in toto*, but there is much we can learn and apply regarding the laws of our mind and the use of our inner power.

Baptism, the subject of these pages, antedates Christianity. People have baptized by fire and by water all over the world. As previously explained, all these ceremonies are symbolic. Baptism is an outward sign of a desired inward grace. The word *grace* means the Love and Wisdom of God. When we sense the reality of spiritual values and apply them in our lives, we are being baptized daily and hourly. The *water* poured on your head in the baptismal ritual represents symbolically the inner cleansing and purification of the conscious and subconscious mind whether the neophyte be sprinkled, doused, immersed, or partly drowned in water. The external act has no real significance unless it is accompanied by an inner change. The inner change is all that matters.

If you find yourself afraid of germs, the weather, people, and conditions, you are not baptized. When really baptized, your eyes are open to God's Truth; His Truth grips you, making you exclaim with a loud voice, "I am Reborn!" When clean inside, you are clean outside. Cleanliness is next to Godliness. All the sacraments deal with the union of your soul with God or the Good. Your savior is the realization of your desire. If sick, health would be your savior. If your mind is full of discord, peace would be your savior. The solution to your problem, whatever it may be, is always your savior. If a man has thought that he was incurable before the idea enters his mind that God can do all things, that the Intelligence which created his body and all its organs can heal it, the mind fixed with this new idea, brings redemption. It is his

Redeemer and a healing follows. Man now dies to the belief that he cannot be healed, and the idea of perfect health seizes his mind. The Infinite Healing Presence responds to his belief and healing follows. His prayer is answered—he is baptized or cleansed of a false belief. Meditate on the idea of health until it becomes a part of your consciousness and you will become full of the feeling of being what you long to be.

Jesus said, "Verily, verily, I say unto thee, Except a man be born again, he cannot see the kingdom of God. Nicodemus saith unto him, How can a man be born when he is old? can he enter the second time into his mother's womb, and be born? Jesus answered, Verily, verily, I say unto thee, Except a man be born of water and of the Spirit, he cannot enter into the kingdom of God." JOHN 3:3–4–5.

Nicodemus represents the type of mind you find everywhere which believes in the strict letter of the scripture; yet he is depicted as seeking the truth; i.e., he is becoming aware of a Divine power within. *Nicodemus* coming to Jesus by night means the average man, governed by his five senses, on awakening to the Truth, turns to the spiritual power within represented by Jesus and begins to digest and absorb heavenly Truths. Nicodemus represents a phase of mind typified by the person who has a particular religious belief just because his parents had such a creed. Nicodemus was a *pharisee*, meaning a person who observes the external forms of religion without any spiritual understanding as to its origin or meaning. Nicodemus thinks that rebirth means being born again of a woman. What he fails to see is that man can enter the second time into the mother's womb symbolically and be reborn spiritually.

It is happening every day all over the world. The *womb* represents the creative mind, consciousness. The average man thinks of God as afar off. He considers Heaven as a place to which he goes after death. In order to perceive what rebirth is, we must discard our religious prejudices, dislikes, and illusions of the senses. *Rebirth* is a higher level of being, a new state of consciousness wherein man begins to think in a new way.

I knew an alcoholic in London who was also a murderer. He had an intense desire to become a new man. His constant prayer was: "God and His love fills my heart and mind." As he began to detach himself from the old way of thinking by meditating on God and His love, a tremendous internal change came over him, a Light came into his eye, he was seized by a Divine Power and lifted up to a higher level of being. He was possessed of an inner peace and tranquility. He had a transformation of the heart and he is now helping others to lead a glorious life. He went into his *mother's womb* the second time; which means that out of his joyous feeling or mood as he prayed came forth the healing, the inner peace which passeth all understanding.

Womb is symbolic of the creative power. What is the creative power? It is consciousness. What is consciousness? What you think, feel, believe, and give internal consent to. Your state of consciousness creates all conditions in your world. Awareness is the only power. Sometimes this is called consciousness. What are you aware of now? Do you say, "I am sad, I am poor, I am inferior, I am sick, etc." You are aware of these states, therefore you create them. On the other hand you can say, "I am strong, I am powerful, I am radiant, I am happy, etc." You can think and feel these moods; you will, of course, create circumstances accordingly. That is called the womb because a child comes forth out of a womb. Your mental children are health, harmony, peace, abundance, love, expression, etc. Your thoughts are your mental children. Thoughts are things. "A man is what he thinks all day long." (Emerson).

Your habitual thinking determines your destiny. The average man (Nicodemus) does not understand that rebirth is a mental and spiritual process, a spiritualization of his entire mentality. I explained to a young motion picture actress how to release her hidden powers, in other words, how to be reborn. She had not been expressing even one-tenth of her ability and talents. She began to imagine several times a day that she was thrilling the audience with the song of God which came forth from her. She began to say, "God sings, thinks, and acts through me." She was focused on her ideal. As she continued to meditate in this way, she finally touched the reality of the state and objectively expressed what she subjectively felt. The real artist came forth out of the womb of consciousness. She washed away the old state of inferiority, guilt, and self-condemnation, and resurrected the qualities of faith, confidence, poise, and balance.

In baptism you go down into the water. This represents also going down into a grave—a dying. As you rise up out of the water in which you are immersed, it represents a rising from the grave—a coming to life, so to speak. When you are baptized, literally speaking, you go through rites representing burial and resurrection. The meaning of the whole thing is that the old man in you dies, and the new man is born. Water in the pond or lake will never cleanse you mentally. The only change that matters is a change of consciousness, a real change in the heart where you begin to think, feel, and act in a new way.

"That which is born of the flesh is flesh; and that which is born of the Spirit is spirit." JOHN 3:6. The word *flesh* represents the world-mind, the race mind, the five-sense-man governed by opinions and false beliefs.

His thinking and mental reactions to life are based on his conditioning. He is a sort of a stereotype machine. He responds automatically and mechanically to everything. His response to the headlines, to politics, to religion, and to people is always the same. Words of others trigger his actions. If you find fault with his political favorite, notice how he reacts. He is born of the flesh. The man who is reborn does not react mechanically and is not a machine. He realizes that news, people, comments, or criticisms cannot disturb him because he knows that he is the only thinker in his universe, and no one has the power to disturb him.

When you have charge of your own thoughts and can order them around as you would employees, how could the other hurt you? You would have to decide to move negatively in thought. I am sure you now see what it is to be reborn.

The word *flesh* confuses so many people. I have met many people both here and in the Orient who believe that the way to overcome the *flesh* means a rigorous discipline, giving up the marriage life, becoming a vegetarian, half-starving the body, and giving up all physical pleasures. Others believe in flagellation and physical tortures of all kinds. It is true that many people who run off into caves—and into the wilderness think they are pleasing God; they hope to reach a higher level of spiritual awareness by such means. It is absolutely foolish to try to bring about a spiritual awakening by eating carrots, leading the life of a hermit, drinking six glasses of water every day, concentrating on a black spot on the wall, or concentrating on the navel. Remember one cardinal tenet of spiritual teaching, and that is, *never start from the external* to purify the mind. Starting only from the external, you are climbing up the wrong way. Start always from the inside. The outside is effect, the inside is cause. Take care of the inside, and the outside will manifest the inside. "As within, so without."

Some people say to me, "I am now denying myself so many things." What some of these well-meaning people mean is that they are denying themselves some of the many comforts of life. They are half-starved, neurotic, and suffering from mental aberrations. Many have separated from their husbands in the belief that they would become holier. They are confused by the word *deny*. God wants you to be happy and have all the joy and comforts of life. Enjoy all the good things of life and all its conveniences. They all come from God. Deny, i.e., reject all emotions which are negative and destructive. Reject (deny) mentally all thoughts unfit for the house of God (your mind). Refuse to indulge in self-pity, recriminations, and feeling sorry for yourself. Deny yourself the pseudo-pleasure of the hurt feeling, the holier than thou attitude, self-justification, spiritual pride, arrogance, conceit, and vanity. Of course, you have to deny yourself in the sense that you will reject anything and everything that does not contribute to your inner peace in the sanctuary of your soul. Observe yourself many times a day and say, "What am I thinking now? What mental company am I keeping?" Check yourself; then begin to keep company with God and His way.

Look at the grub worm. Notice the metamorphosis which takes place there. Through this internal change it takes on wings and becomes a butterfly. Wings were not added on—the transformation reveals what was always there. Your wings are your thought and feeling enabling you to soar aloft and rest in the Secret Place of the Most High, beyond time and space, secure in that Impregnable Fortress, that Invincible Citadel. In that inner sanctuary you may meditate on the reality of your desire by sensing it and feeling it; and whatever you imagine and feel, you will become and will experience. This is called by Troward "self-contemplation of the spirit." Spirit feels itself to be a certain thing; then it becomes what it feels itself to be.

In another place Troward says, "Feeling is the law and the law is the feeling, the law of perfect creativeness." It is the feeling of the game, the feeling of the horse, the feeling of the artist, the feeling of the musician, the feeling of the man in prayer. Go now into that "sweet hour of prayer" and feel the reality of your desire, and the water in you—your consciousness will flow into manifestation (water and the spirit), (consciousness and feeling). "Be not fashioned according to the world but be ye transformed by the renewal of your mind." ROMANS 12:2.

The fertilized ovum becomes a man; this is a form of transformation. The seed becomes a true likeness. When the Bible speaks of baptism and transformation, it refers to a psychological and emotional transformation. You really live with your thoughts, feelings, beliefs, emotions, moods, images, concepts, and dreams all day long. The new interpretation of life is the real baptism. When a person is truly baptized, there is a mark on his soul which cannot be wiped out. Divine love is indelibly written in the heart and tongue also. God has put His mark upon you. You now reveal His light and love in all your ways. "Wist ye not that I must be about my Father's business?" LUKE 2:49.

Baptism, or healing through prayer, was practiced in the Old Testament also. In the book of *II Kings*, Chapter 5, we read of a great Syrian called Naaman who was leprous. The maid to Naaman's wife told her that the prophet Elisha could heal her husband. Naaman went to see Elisha "and Elisha sent a messenger unto him saying, Go and wash in Jordan seven times, and thy flesh shall come again to thee, and thou

shalt be clean." II Kings 5:10. The Bible says Naaman
was wroth. He expected the prophet to place his
hands on him and heal him. His servants persuaded
him to carry out the command of Elisha. "Then went
he down, and dipped himself seven times in Jordan,
according to the saying of the man of God: and his
flesh came again like unto the flesh of a little child and
he was clean." II Kings 5:14.

A purely literal interpretation of this story would
be too absurd for words. A psychological interpretation, which is what is intended, fills the soul with joy.
Any man who is completely attached to the material
world, and believes causation is external, is leprous in
the biblical sense, *i.e.,* he is unclean and unholy. Any
man with a problem is Naaman. It means the conscious, reasoning mind which is now ready to agree
that there is a Divine, Healing, Omnipotent Power
and he wants to unite with it. *Elisha* means God is salvation or the presence of God in you is the solution
to your problem. The little *maiden* mentioned means
spiritual perception or the awakening of the mind to
spiritual values.

To wash in the Jordan seven times symbolically represents a cleansing of the mind through the baptism
of spiritual thought. The Jordan means the subconscious mind which is influenced negatively and positively also. In man's ignorance and unredeemed state

it is muddy with false concepts and turbulent with materiality and sense-evidence. This negative stream lodged in the subconscious, which is the cause of all disease and pain, must be cleansed by scientific prayer symbolized by washing seven times. When the subconscious is cleansed of the false belief, a healing follows. Hatred, the guilt feeling, resentment, jealousy, and other destructive emotions dam up the free flow of Divine energy and healing grace cutting off the flow of God's love and health. *Jordan* could be called the race mind which flows through all of us. Actually, we are all immersed in the race mind or collective unconscious, as Carl Jung calls it.

Naaman was commanded to bathe seven times; this means to contemplate the Infinite Healing Presence within you knowing that this Living Intelligence which made you is now making you whole and perfect; then you are actually immersed in the Holy Omnipresence. You have gone to God within formless, faceless, all bliss, joy, peace, and beauty. There are no divisions or quarrels there. You are in Heaven where all is bliss, harmony, and peace. You have gone in meditation to Him who sent you. Here in the secret place of prayer you meditate on the perfect healing until you succeed in obtaining a vivid realization concerning it. The *seventh sprinkle* of water, or the *seventh plunge*, means the point of complete mental acceptance or conviction. The seventh sprinkle means the length of time it takes you to reach a conviction in your mind that your prayer is answered. The seventh sprinkle means the mind is stilled and fixed in the realization that you are now made whole or that you really possess that which you desire to possess.

As you fully and completely accept the idea of perfect health, you have immersed yourself seven times in the water and you feel no need or desire to pray further on the matter. You are satisfied and mentally you have a sense of inner certitude and deep abiding satisfaction. This is the seventh day, the seventh hour, the seventh sprinkle, the seventh bath, etc. Regardless of the malady, whether leprosy, tuberculosis, malignancy, growth, etc., you can now play the role of Naaman and be baptized spiritually by turning your attention completely away from the problem or involvement and place all your attention and devotion on your goal, ideal, or objective. As you begin to feel that an Almighty Power is responding in your behalf, confidence and faith will be generated. Continue to preserve, to bathe mentally in that holy feeling, the feeling of wholeness and perfection, until the day breaks and the shadows flee away.

In closing we will comment on the ritual and ceremony of baptism. Sponsors at baptism are like a regent who rules for the boy king until he comes of age. Likewise, the child needs the spiritual care and protection of parents until it can take care of its spiritual powers. We call such a person a sponsor or godparent. In ancient times there was constant danger of death by persecutions and parents designated others to watch over the spiritual needs of their children in case they should die or meet with martyrdom. Sponsors make a profession of faith in the name of the child. Primarily, of course, the duty belongs to the parents. Parents become true sponsors for the child only when they pledge themselves seriously to surround the child with a happy, joyous, Godlike, spiritual atmosphere. When the father and mother keep their thoughts, feelings, and conversation upon the beautiful, the elevating, the dignifying, the loving, and the noble things of life, the child subconsciously receives the spiritual influence or mood and grows in the image and likeness of the dominant spiritual atmosphere. The child is now being baptized hourly and daily. If, however, parents quarrel, fight, resent each other; if they dwell on the limited, morbid experiences of life, there is no baptism for the child, regardless of all the ceremonies in the world. Parents should pray together for the child. Their thoughts should be centered on God's Eternal Love, Supply, Harmony, and Peace. Their mood should be the joyous expectancy of the best and nothing but the best. The child should be always dedicated to God and to His expression only. The child should be taught as soon as possible that he is a child of God and that God dwells in him. The home should be a dwelling place for God so that whoever enters says in his heart, "Surely God is in this place."

The sponsor in Baptism makes three solemn pledges to renounce Satan. The priest says, "Joseph, dost thou renounce Satan?"

Through the sponsors come the answer, "I do renounce him."

The priest says, "And all his works?"

Again the sponsors answer, "I do renounce him."

A third question, "And all his pomp?"

And the third reply, "I do renounce him."

The word *Satan* or *Devil*, refers to negative thoughts, negative imagery of any kind. It means that you reject all destructive talking and thinking in the presence of the child, and keep your mind as a tabernacle of the Most High. Satan is the adversary or all the adverse thoughts that come into your mind, such as beliefs in and fear of sickness, pain, misfortune, other powers, and other gods. Fear is your adversary. When you pray, you turn away from fear which is nothing trying to be something, and you contemplate the solution, the way out, the answer. You devote all your attention to the answer; then you get a lift in consciousness and the spirit flows in response. You remain in that fixed state and the answer will come. You have cast out fear by entering into the mood of faith and confidence in an Almighty Power which is One and Indivisible. You have cast out Satan or the negative thought or image and supplanted it with the positive goal or ideal you wished to achieve. You renounce the Devil or Satan when you give up the belief in two powers, in two gods, and place all your faith and trust in the One Power and Presence.

"Hear, O Israel: The Lord our God is one Lord." DEUTERONOMY 6:4. Satan is the accuser. Have you ever accused yourself, blamed yourself for the mistakes you have made? that is Satan. Cease this destructive attitude. Turn to things Spiritual and Divine, to some constructive work, and move forward in the Light. Get busy about your Father's business. When busy on God's business, you have no time to moan, cry, whimper, whine, and condemn.

"I beheld Satan as lightning fall from heaven." LUKE 10:18. Heaven is your mind at peace. When your mind is disturbed by the adversary (the adverse thought) there is Satan and war in heaven. Realize that the negative, as Troward says, is the absence of good, completely devoid of power as there is no principle to back it up, with nothing to sustain it; only the positive and the affirmative are real. When you assert the positive position, mentally coming to a clear-cut decision in your mind, Satan falls from heaven (error falls away). It falls as lightning, meaning the energy behind the negative thought is completely dissipated and destroyed in the same way that lightning explodes and wastes its energy.

The works and pomp renounced by the sponsor mean errors of all kind. Pomp refers to the vanity, conceit, and sham of the world. Pomp is an empty show. What is the use of putting on an act on the outside? It is what you think and feel inside that matters. Your words may belie your inner feeling. How do you feel about people in their absence? How do you meet people in your mind? That is the acid test of your inner state of consciousness. Your politeness on the surface is important. Are you polite when you meet them in your mind? If you resent them in your mind, you have not renounced Satan. You alone are responsible for the way you think about people. You are the thinker in your own world.

Dressed in a beautiful, white surplice, a sign of purity, and in a purple stole, a sign of spiritual authority, the priest or minister tells the child to keep the commandments and love God. Then he breathes gently three times across the face of the child praying, "Depart from him, thou unclean spirit, and give place to the Holy Ghost, the paraclete." The *unclean spirits* are, as you know, the negative emotions of the parent. The *Holy Ghost* means God's Wisdom. You remember, Mary was pregnant with the Holy Ghost, symbolizing the subjective nature full of the Wisdom, Intelligence, and Power of God. All of us must give place to the Holy Ghost (Wisdom) if we wish to come out of the race mind (original sin). When you know that you are what you think all day long; when you realize that what you feel, you experience and attract; when you know that a change of feeling is a change of destiny, and that consciousness is the only cause and creative power in your world, you have received the Holy Ghost, the paraclete, and you are ready to blend your conscious and subconscious mind harmoniously and synchronously. You will now choose only from the Infinite Reservoir of Good or God.

The priest or minister makes the sign of the cross on the forehead and breast of the infant, a little salt is placed on the tongue, and the hand of the priest is placed on the child's head. Salt is a preservative, giving taste to food. You are to taste the sweet savor of the Truths of God and keep them forever lodged and preserved in the repository of the faithful breast. The *sign of the cross* means crossing over from darkness to light, from confusion to peace, from ignorance to wisdom. Whenever you pray, you make the sign of the cross which is the impression of your new ideal in consciousness, and this impression becomes an expression. You have crossed over from the limited state to the freedom state. Your desire for wealth can be achieved by making the sign of the cross, which is psychological and figurative, by entering into the spirit of opulence and living in that mood of wealth until you convey the idea of wealth to your subconscious; then your idea or desire for wealth has crossed from conscious mind to subconscious mind; the sign is completed.

In making the sign of the cross you say, "In the name of the Father, the Son, and the Holy Ghost, Amen." The *name* means the nature of God, a complete recognition of God as the source or fountain of all good. The *Son* is your desire. The *Holy Ghost* is your feeling of being what you long to be, or the feeling of oneness with your ideal. The *sign of the cross* is the perfect formula for prayer. All it means is recognition, acceptance, and conviction. Look to God as source and cause. Accept your desire and walk in the feeling it is yours until you reach the point of peace of conviction within yourself; that is the sign of the cross. Isn't that beautiful?

The upright beam of the cross represents I AM or God. The transverse beam is your concept or estimate of yourself. What is your concept of yourself? Your concept of God determines your whole future, your entire destiny. Your concept of yourself is really your concept of God. The circle depends on the length of diameter. Increase the diameter and you increase the size of the circle. Enlarge the estimate of yourself. Get a new, lofty, exalted concept of yourself. Realize you are a son of God, heir to all of God's Wisdom, Truth, and Beauty. Live in that new mental atmosphere; then your circle of happiness, peace, joy, and abundance will magnify and multiply a thousandfold. Your desert will rejoice and blossom as the rose.

The priest pours water three times in the form of a cross on the head of the child repeating the words, "I baptize you in the name of the Father, the Son, and the Holy Ghost." The esoteric or hidden meaning of this is an explanation of the three aspects of Universal Spirit by the power of which all things are made, and there is nothing that is not made by that power. Hydrogen and oxygen electrolyzed produce water. A seed, the creative essence, and the soil brings forth the fruit. You find the trinity everywhere—man, wife, and child; idea, feeling and manifestation; thought, emotion, and conviction. The third element of the metaphysician is peace and God is Peace. When the conscious mind and the subconscious mind synchronize and agree with the idea or desire, the cross is completed.

The Father could be called your conscious mind which selects the idea or desire. The subjective feeling or emotional nature is that which receives the idea or desire through feeling. The male, or conscious mind, impresses the female, or subconscious mind, with the idea. The expression is made manifest and is the image and likeness of the impression. The son testifies or bears witness to his father and mother (idea and feeling); this is the Triune God—the Father, the Son, and the Holy Ghost.

The crown of the head is anointed in the form of a cross with oil of chrism. *Oil* represents illumination and healing. Chrism or Chrismia means Anointed One or Christos. The oil represents a union or sense of wholeness, a covenant with God. It means the intellect is now governed and anointed by the wisdom of God. You are now sanctified and a participant of God's Inner Wisdom which comes forth from the Treasure House of Eternity.

The child is offered a lighted candle. That is to remind him that he is to let his light so shine upon men that they shall see his good works, thereby glorifying his Father which is in Heaven. You are here to bring forth Wisdom, Light, Love, Peace, and Beauty. You are here to express more and more of God. "Receive this burning Light and keep thy baptism so as to be without blame." Observe the commandment of God that, when our Lord shall come to His wedding feast, thou mayest meet Him and live forever and ever. Go in peace and God be with you.

2

Learn How to Make Your Dreams Come True

Confirmation

Every *sacrament* is an act of Divine union, resulting in a deeper downpour of grace—a sense of deep conviction of things spiritual beyond mere words. Every true prayer is a *sacrament* for it means uniting with your desire. Every desire or idea has its own fragrance; as you meditate on it, you will secrete a perfume, a joy, an inner fragrance which is a deep feeling of satisfaction. When you feast on your desire and call forth the mood, or the full feeling, your desire and feeling become one. Prayer is really a marriage ceremony as you are told in "The Marriage Feast of Cana."*

---

* See Chapter 2, *How to Attract Money.*

When fear departs from your consciousness, it is the sign that you are really partaking of the various sacraments and entering into a state of grace and deep spiritual conviction. Jesus said that an adulterous generation ever seeks for an outward sign; none shall be given, but the sign of Jonah. The word *Jonah* means conviction, the idea felt as true. You must impregnate the subconscious (the whale) with your desire or idea through feeling; then a new Jonah (a new man) will come forth out of the whale (consciousness) clothed in the new desire.

All the stories in the Bible, as well as all the sacraments, deal with the relationship between the male and female principle within each of us. Another way of saying it is that our prayers deal with the proper, harmonious interrelationship between the objective and subjective nature of man. Dare to become lost in the joy of being what you long to be. You can become so identified with your desire or ideal that all else is blotted out, and you are alone with your fulfilled desire.

One Bible student who took our classes on the inner meaning of the Book of Revelation and the Book of John told me recently that his young brother ran away from home with another boy. His mother was heartbroken. They couldn't find him anywhere. He stilled the wheels of his mind, touched his young brother's head and stroked his hair (all in his imagination); then he embraced his brother saying, "It's wonderful to have you back. You love your mother, don't you?" He did this easily, quietly, and lovingly. He was completely relaxed about it all and enjoyed the mental drama. When he opened his eyes, he told me he was amazed that his brother wasn't there, it was all so real, so natural, and so vivid. Meaning that he had fixed the state subjectively, that Jonah (his desire for his brother) had entered the subconscious (the belly of the whale), and lo and behold, the new Jonah came forth. His brother came home the next day. He said that he got as far as Phoenix, Arizona, when a compelling urge came over him to return home to his mother; this was the subjective wisdom which acted upon his mind causing him to return home.

You experience the sacrament of confirmation when you sense a feeling of rest from striving—a feeling that after all you no longer want or seek the state, since subjectively you feel your prayer is answered. The state is confirmed or felt as true. There is always a let down or sense of relaxation and peace when you succeed in impressing your desire subconsciously. When the spiritual creative act has been accomplished you cry, "It is finished!" You have succeeded in crossing over to a subjective level. You have died on the cross; i.e., you have left the old state and crossed over to the new state—the answered prayer.

Every answered prayer is a process of crucifixion. I don't know why we should dodge the issue; let us begin to teach it and get rid of all metaphysical superstitions about crucifixion and resurrection. In our chapter on "Holy Communion" we learn that Jesus looked upon bread as a concept of consciousness and not any conditioned form. We learn also about the chemistry of alimentation, its inner significance and its miraculous implications. Eat what you wish, what is good for you, and what agrees with you. Be sure you do not become a neurotic or food faddist. Food, such as carrots, bananas, and grapes will not make you more divine. In this doctrine or sacrament of confirmation, you must remember that its real inner significance is the absolute belief in One God without any mental reservations. Do you really look to the One Source for your heaven on earth? Do you really understand the power of consciousness? When you can answer "Yes" to these questions you are really confirmed.

Confirmation is an outward sign of a desired inward grace—a sensing of the reality of spiritual values. The church refers to confirmation as a sacrament which makes you a strong and perfect Christian. We should understand that the word *Christian* applies to anyone who uses the principle of life constructively. It does not refer to beliefs or personalities. The outward sign of confirmation is the laying on of the bishop's hands, the anointing with oil, and the repetition of certain prayers. The inward grace is the real sacrament. The church refers to the *Acts of the Apostles* as its authority for the sacrament of confirmation. "Then laid they their hands on them, and they received the Holy Ghost." ACTS 8:17. "Now when the apostles which were at Jerusalem heard that Samaria had received the word of God, they sent unto them Peter and John: Who, when they were come down, prayed for them, that they might receive the Holy Ghost." ACTS 8:14–15.

The material in the *Acts of the Apostles* may have some historical basis but much meat for the soul can be found therein if you will strive to discern behind every name of a personage, city, town, or country a state of consciousness, negative or positive. When it speaks of Saul dying, it means the five-sense, unholy-minded man dying to that state of consciousness and the Paul (little Christ) state of consciousness being born. In other words, you, the reader of this book, are Paul, meaning your intellect is illumined by an interior light, and you know your I AM (life) is God in you. Your own awareness is the God-Presence. Death and life are always going on in your mind. Paul said, "I die daily," meaning he was constantly dying to erroneous concepts, negative ideas, and resurrecting continuously more of God's wisdom, truth, and beauty.

Nothing can be born without something dying. That is why the crucifixion (crossing over) drama is forever taking place. You are always transcending former states. Peter (faith in God) and John (love of God) prayed for them that they might receive the Holy Ghost. These qualities are within you; when faith and love join forces, you truly enter into the Temple Beautiful (high spiritual consciousness) through the Gates Beautiful (conscious mind).

Through faith you become strong. *Faith* is going in one direction only, believing in One Power—the Spiritual Power within. You love God in the sense that you feel your oneness with Him, and you give the Spiritual Power your supreme allegiance, devotion, and loyalty. You are true to It alone. The sacrament of confirmation means that you are absolutely convinced that there is but one power and one cause—your own consciousness. You no longer give power to stars, the weather, other people, germs, external powers, entities, etc. You have dispensed with all secondary gods and powers. Confirmation takes place in your own mind and heart—it is purely psychological and has nothing to do with external rites or ceremonies. You have absolutely come to the point once and for all. You have made a definite, concrete decision. You have mapped out your future destiny. You know where you are going. You are no longer adrift on the ocean of life.

On the pathway of life you will now keep your eye on the beam.

Here is a test to see if you have advanced to the degree of consciousness called confirmation: If you pray for a healing and say, "I can't be healed" or "I'm incurable," you are identifying and acknowledging other powers. You are denying the One True God. The minute you place a suppositional opposite in your mind to the One Power, you have not yet advanced to this level of consciousness called confirmation. To say, "I can't make ends meet," "There is no way out," "It is hopeless," "He is uncurable," "I will lose everything," "A jinx is following me," or anything similar to them, you are mentally and emotionally uniting with negativity. You are not being loyal, true, devoted to the ONE POWER, your own I AMNESS. If you really believed, you would not mentally unite with these false concepts; this is called idolatry or in the Bible adultery. Idolatry and adultery are synonymous in biblical terminology. *To worship* is to give attention to, to exalt, to deem worthy of study and devotion.

To illustrate what true confirmation is: I was talking to a young Japanese boy during my lectures in Japan last year. He said that he had been sentenced to be shot during the war; he added that he had been accused falsely, but all that is beside the point. The point is, he called Peter (faith in God) and John (love and at-one-ment with the One True God—The One Power) and said boldly to himself, "I can't be shot. I am a son of God. God can't shoot Himself." He kept repeating the words of the 91st Psalm. He wrote them in his heart. He knew there was only One Power. He was released with no explanations and told to go back to duty.

The Bible refers to the angel of the Lord which means a vivid insight and conviction in the Power of God enabling man to free himself from any limitation. When we are inclined to waver and doubt, when faced with a difficult situation, let us ask ourselves, "Where is my faith, what is the truth, what do I believe in?" The answer will steal over our minds like the dew of Heaven, and we will feel that our faith and trust are of God—omnipotent and able to save us like the faith of the Japanese boy who knew he could not be shot.

Your knowledge of Truth is being forever put to the test. Are there not times in your life when you had the fear that perhaps all this metaphysical business is simply barren dialectics and sophistry? But the Job state of mind comes to our aid, and like Joshua of old, we stand firm in the I AM state of mind, resting in God and His law. This state of mind bids the sun (conscious mind) to stand still and see the salvation of the Lord. The latter means the solution which the subjective wisdom will bring to pass as we turn our request over to it and trust it implicitly.

"Whom say ye that I am?" What answer do you give to this? Why not tell the truth and say, "I am a son of the living God." Until you do this, the world will take you but at your own low estimate and evaluation of yourself. You must find the hiding place of Divinity in your own household. We must avoid all deification of personalities when considering the sacraments. Jesus said, "Why call thou me good?" Only the Father is good—"He doeth the works." There is much allegory in the Bible, but these allegorizations do not necessarily destroy geographical and historical backgrounds. All cities such as Los Angeles, New York, San Francisco, Cairo, etc., take on a personality and quality of their own. Each city has a subjective feel based on the mental atmosphere of the inhabitants of the city. The same applies to personages, such as Paul, Jesus, Moses, Isaiah, Lincoln, or Washington who left their marks in human destiny. In other words allegory does not destroy history, but serves to enrich it. Today we say, "going to Munich" or "another Korea." How meaningful have become popular phrases and places, such as "another red herring," "spirit of Geneva," etc.

If you have seen the play, *Lincoln,* I am sure you know that the writer of the play makes Lincoln say and do whatever he wanted in order to complete the drama or story. Likewise it does not mean that some of the characters in the Bible were not real, but the writers undoubtedly wrote a drama of truth around them portraying the results of states of consciousness. All stories in the Bible, therefore, are stories about everyone, about you.

In the sacrament of confirmation you are to be a witness to reality; i.e., you are to reflect the hidden beauty of God; then, with Jesus, you can well declare, "He that hath seen me, hath seen the Father." You are firmly convinced of One Power and you say "Nay" to all else. When confirmed, in the true psychological sense of the word, you are completely finished with superficial, ritualistic religion, mere religious dialectics, and semantics which get you nowhere in the truth. Mere mouthings of the words "Jesus Christ," "blood of the lamb," "the cross of Christ," etc., will avail you nothing unless you understand the meaning of these words. The external beliefs associated with these words represent rank nonsense and superstition.

You must be baptized before confirmation, which means that before the birth of Jesus (your awareness of God or I AM in you), you were John baptizing with water. John the Baptist came to the world wearing a leather girdle (disciplining of emotions), eating wild honey and locusts, and striking the axe to the root of the trees (false systems of religious beliefs). He represents you at the time you first turned away from religious beliefs. At first you felt like a pioneer preaching with great fire and zest. All of us pass through this sophomoric state. After a while we calm down or settle down and we begin preaching to the one who needs it most—ourselves.

In prayer or treatment, if you want to help another, turn your mind completely toward God; this is the first step in the treatment process. The second step is to contemplate the solution of the problem (the answer). Do this frequently until you arrive at a conviction. This is symbolized by Jesus in the Scriptures who is "the one who should come" or the manifestation of your ideal. Your desire objectified is your Jesus—your solution. Jesus and Joshua are identical in the Bible, both mean God is the savior or emancipator. In another sense Jesus represents the Truth which, when it ascends into working consciousness in a man, begins a series of acts which are the result of the descent of Holy (whole) spirit.

In confirmation you receive the Holy Ghost which means that you no longer have a blind faith but a living, dynamic vibrant faith in the God-power and wisdom within. When your intellect becomes convinced of the wonderful idea that you are a son of God and heir to all of God's riches; when you feel the truth of this all through your whole being; the Holy Spirit (spirit of oneness with God) has come upon you in all its power and majesty, and there is no longer any need for John (conscious mind, reasoning, intellect). Your confirmation is complete because your feeling of conviction of God's Presence takes over and leads you into the Holy of Holies within. Historically, it is quite possible that an illumined man who was a real student of the Holy Way or Holy Path did study in Egyptian and Indian esoteric schools, waxed strong in wisdom, and the healings attributed to him. This person, Jesus, also became an allegorization of the process in divine alchemy and transformation.

After receiving confirmation you are told that you are now a soldier of Christ. What does this mean? It means that your goal as a soldier is to be loyal to Truth and to God's Laws of Love, Order, Beauty, and Proportion, which means that you refuse to dwell mentally on ideas extraneous and contrary to your announced objective as a soldier of the One Who Forever Is. You are a soldier of God when you follow out the orders and instructions you have received. You learned that you can overcome all problems through prayer, that the principle within will lift you above any experience and set you on the highroad to freedom and peace of mind; furthermore, you know and believe that there is a scientific way of prayer which brings results. Knowing this, you have turned over a new leaf; you are on the way to victory over all things in your life. As a good and loyal soldier, you will always respond to your faith in God. You are aware that the subjective area of your mind responds to your mode of thought; therefore, you watch carefully to see to it that only Godlike concepts and ideas enter in. As a soldier you stand guard at the doorway of your mind, absolutely refusing permission of entry to any negative, limiting ideas or moods. You are always on duty. You are never off guard. By day and by night you are constantly on guard duty fully armed to resist all aggressors.

To be confirmed in the church, you must know the chief truths of your religion. In psychological parlance, you must know how your conscious and subconscious mind function. Up to and including the tenth century, it was the custom to confer confirmation on children after baptism. But that custom has been discontinued to a great extent as the person is supposed to understand his religion. The reason you must have been baptized before you can receive confirmation is simply this, "Wisdom will not enter into a malicious soul." WISDOM 1:4. You must cleanse and wash your mind of false beliefs and erroneous concepts to receive the wisdom or true knowledge of God. True knowledge of God is confirmation. All those confirmed add to their names, usually the name of some saint. Name means nature, and the addition of another name really means a new state of consciousness. The name you take is supposed to be a model and protector for you.

You have heard the expression, "his nature is to be happy." This means he has appropriated the consciousness of happiness. He has made it a habit to be happy, having chosen through constructive imagery and thinking. The qualities of happiness were appropriated by him and he expresses happiness. "Whatever ye shall ask in my name" means if you enter into the victorious, triumphant state of consciousness, you will receive. When you say your name is Mary Jones, this denotes everything about you, your characteristics, disposition, the fact you are a woman, your age, nationality, education, size, financial and social status, and all things appertaining to you. Your name completely identifies you. The new name you receive at confirmation represents, therefore, a new awareness, a greater knowledge of the Truth of God, a greater understanding which the name represents. All this is lost to the candidate for confirmation. It is another ceremony in his life without understanding. The bishop, in a beautiful ceremony, says to the candidate for confirmation, "May the Holy Ghost (feeling of oneness with God) come upon you and the Power of the Most High keep you from sins, Amen." The word *amen* means the union or agreement of the conscious or subconscious mind which is answered prayer. If there is any argument or doubt in your deeper mind as to the truth of that which you affirm consciously, there is no real amen. Keep on persevering and agreement will be reached.

The bishop prays that wisdom, understanding, guidance, fortitude, and knowledge of Godliness be given to all those confirmed. The bishop, seated at the altar, dips the thumb of his right hand in the holy chrism, that is, the oil with balm, places his hand on the boy's head and makes the sign of the cross with the oil on his forehead saying, "I sign thee with the sign of the cross and I confirm thee with the chrism of salvation in the name of the Father, Son, and Holy Ghost." Then the bishop strikes the child confirmed gently on the cheek saying, "Peace be with you." The blow on the cheek is to remind the person confirmed that he is to be patient, knowing that in peace and in confidence lie his strength. The oil used is the perfumed oil which has been consecrated on Holy Thursday. Holy Thursday precedes Good Friday meaning the day of God's Love, or the moment when you become one with your prayer or ideal; then you have died to the old state and you have resurrected a new state of consciousness. Holy Thursday is the day when the oil is consecrated and is purely symbolic. *Holy Thursday* means an exalted state of mind, a high place in consciousness, a place of peace and love. When you succeed in becoming one with your desire, a wave of peace steals over you, and the mental and spiritual love act is completed, symbolizing the ritual of Holy Thursday and Good Friday (day of love). The old man is now dead. The new, subjective state is ready for resurrection; this is all a process of prayer. The *sign of the cross with oil* means that you have crossed over to a higher state of consciousness. The *forehead* is symbolic of knowledge and understanding. The *oil* bespeaks a greater measure of light and wisdom. The perpendicular beam of the cross means God—I AM, consciousness, awareness. It means the Timeless One within all of us. The transverse beam of the cross represents your conception, estimate, or blueprint of yourself. That is the sign of the cross or your real concept of yourself. Your concept of yourself is your concept of God which determines your whole life. The transverse beam represents time and space also. The transverse beam of the cross represents past, present, and future. There is no growth in time. Don't say things will be better next year or five years from now. Your condition, circumstances, and experience will not improve or change for the better until you ascend to a higher level of consciousness represented by the perpendicular beam of the cross which is timeless and spaceless. Your spiritual growth and advancement has

nothing to do with time and space. Rise in consciousness by contemplating the qualities and attributes of
God and you become what you contemplate. Your
transverse beam is then placed higher on the perpendicular beam. In other words you have ascended to
another level of consciousness. That is the meaning
of placing the sign of the cross on your forehead with
the holy oil.

You realize, of course, that you do not ascend to
a higher level of consciousness until you begin to
transform yourself by daily prayer and meditation. It
is not something that is conferred on you by another.
The external ritual and ceremony, while beautiful
and uplifting, may induce a happy, joyous, emotional
reaction, but the only real, worth-while change is the
internal change of the heart where the man becomes a
new man in all his ways.

The *chrism of salvation* means that the chrism or
perfumed oil is your solution. Salvation means solution. Chrism is perfumed oil which we have referred
to and it means that Love and Wisdom solves all problems. *Wisdom* means the right thought. *Love* means
the emotional attachment to the right thought, idea,
plan, or purpose. That is all it means and that is all it
ever meant. All these rituals and ceremonies, such as
anointing with oil and making the sign of the cross
refer to psychological changes in man; or to use bib-

lical language, they refer to the descent of the Holy Spirit in man.

"The Spirit of the Lord is upon me, because he hath anointed me to preach the gospel to the poor; he hath sent me to heal the brokenhearted, to preach deliverance to the captives, and recovering of sight to the blind, to set at liberty them that are bruised." Luke 4:18. "This day is the scripture fulfilled in your ears." Luke 4:21. Here Jesus is telling you that God or your Good is the Eternal Now. This very moment you can claim your good, such as peace, harmony, health, or true place, and the Spirit of the Lord is upon you meaning the mood of faith and confidence in an Almighty Power which never fails. This feeling of confidence and trust in the Spiritual Power sinks down into your mind and heart, lifts you up, fires your imagination, and kindles your faith, enabling you to fulfill your desire now, today.

Now is the day of salvation. Some people say to me, "O some day I will be happy," or "Some time in the future I shall have a healing." The healing principle is within you now. Use it this moment. Why say, "Some day I will pay all my bills." Go within and claim that the spirit of opulence is manifesting itself now in all your affairs. Believe it, accept it, and watch the great drama of God in operation. Don't postpone your happiness. Choose happiness now. Happiness is a habit.

Make it a habit to be happy by choosing wholesome, constructive, joyous, and loving thoughts and imagery all day long. The peace of God is within. Why say, "Some day peace will come." Tune in on the God of Peace and announce in the temple of your own consciousness the presence of peace, health, happiness, and abundance. They are waiting for you now. You take them according to law, and the law is "I am that which I contemplate." Troward says, "All things are made by the self-contemplation of spirit." You are that which you feel yourself to be. The feeling of wealth produces wealth now. The feeling of strength produces strength. The feeling of health produces health. Whatever you mentally identify yourself with and feel as true becomes a reality in your world. You have now found your savior in the temple of your own consciousness. Open the door today to a new life. Why postpone your experience of God. God is the Eternal Now. "This day is the Scripture fulfilled in your ears."

"And suddenly there came a sound from heaven as of a rushing, mighty wind, and it filled all the house where they were sitting. And there appeared unto them cloven tongues like as of fire, and it sat upon each of them. And they were all filled with the Holy Ghost, and began to speak with other tongues, as the Spirit gave them utterance." Acts 2:2–3–4. When you subjectively feel as true what your reason and senses deny, you are filled with the Holy Ghost or Whole Spirit, meaning you are integrated or one piece. You no longer have a divided mind. You and your desire are one. You now speak in a foreign tongue, meaning the new affirmation, the new realization. You speak in a new tongue when you are happy, joyous, full of love, and good will. The word *tongue* means your mood, tone, feeling, and mental attitude. The Bible says "These men are full of new wine." ACTS 2:13. This means you are filled full of the feeling of being what you long to be. You can begin now and speak in a new tongue. If resentful, pour out the spirit of forgiveness, love, and good will. Pray for the other. Bless him. You are speaking in a new language—the language of God.

In what language does God speak? Not in Hebrew, Greek, or Gaelic. The language of God is sometimes referred to as the Still Small Voice, the voice of intuition whereby you are taught from within. The language of God is also the mood of Love, Joy, Beauty, and Peace. The unfoldment of the spiritual power within you is the gift of tongues. The tongues of fire represent the intelligence of God coming into your mind. *The sound from heaven* which you hear is the sound of your answered prayer. The *mighty wind* means the wave of peace which steals over your mind when you experience the joy of the answered prayer. When you read the second chapter of the *Acts of the Apostles* it says, "And when the day of Pentecost was fully come, they were all with one accord in one place." Acts 2:1.

Let us enact this whole drama within ourselves now. The *day of Pentecost* means the day of feasting. Prayer is a feast at which you eat of your idea until you are one with it. One of our students recently heard from the teacher of his boy that his son was dull and backward, and should be sent to a special school. This father began to get lost in the joy of hearing the opposite. Every night he would imagine his son showing him his report card and saying, "Daddy, I received all A's." He kept this up until it became a living conviction. His boy blossomed forth and is one of the best students in his class. Pentecost means the fruit of the idea on which you meditate; this is exactly what the father experienced. The father's prayer caused the intelligence and wisdom of God to well up in the mind of the boy, and he fulfilled his father's conviction of him. "They were all together in one place." This means to sit down, relax, stop the wheels of your mind, and concentrate all your faculties and thought forces on the spiritual power within; then focus all your attention on your ideal. As you do this, you will find an exhilaration of the whole man similar to that produced by wine. You are "filled with new wine."

As you busy your mind along these lines you will succeed in qualifying your consciousness with your ideal. When your prayer is answered, you speak in a new tongue. The man who was poverty-stricken and is now rolling in wealth is speaking in a new tongue. The man who was crippled with arthritis and now walks the earth a free man is speaking and proclaiming to the world the new tongue of health, faith in God, and His Healing Presence. He has received the Holy Ghost (whole spirit) a feeling of wholeness, of health, and peace of mind. The Bible says Moses "poured the oil of unction upon Aaron's head and he anointed and consecrated him." LEVITICUS 8:12. *The oil of unction* contained perfumed spices which were mixed with oils such as myrrh, cinnamon, and cassia. *Moses* means the subjective wisdom and intelligence of the deeper mind. *Aaron* is the intellect or the conscious mind. The *oil of unction* refers to the wisdom of God which illumines the intellect of man; then he is said to be anointed and consecrated. Pouring oil is a figurative and metaphorical expression. It is the language of the Bible which must be seen in a psychological sense to have any real meaning.

The word *Messias* is but a transcript of the Hebrew word *Messiah*. The word *Christos* is a translation into Greek of the same term which means anointed. You will read such terms as these in theological books: Chrism of salvation, chrism of spiritual ointment, perfume, perfume of perfection. All these terms mean the same thing, namely illumined reason. The oil used is olive oil symbolic of cheerfulness and thanksgiving. "Behold, how good and how pleasant it is for brethren to dwell together in unity! It is like the precious ointment upon the head, that ran down upon the beard, even Aaron's beard." PSALMS 133:1–2. "Ointment and perfume rejoice the heart: so doth the sweetness of a man's friend." PROVERBS 27:9.

Outer things such as oil, ointment, perfume, etc., are used to portray the grace, the beauty, and the love of God operating in the mind and heart of man. You have noticed the odor of the garden after the rain. You have smelled the sweet perfume of the rose and you have smelled the briny ocean. Is it not through the sense of smell that we communicate with the beauty of the world all about us? Likewise, we are to inhale the perfume of Divinity by meditating on whatsoever things are true, whatsoever things are lovely and of good report. You cannot suppress the perfume of a rose; neither can you suppress the joy which arises in you as you enter into the realization of the answered prayer. "How much better is thy love than wine! and the smell of thine ointments than all spices! Thy lips, O my spouse, drop as the honeycomb: honey and milk are under thy tongue; and the smell of thy garments is like the smell of Lebanon." SONG OF SOLOMON 4:10–11.

Here the inspired writer is telling you how to pray and he likens it to a romance with a woman. When you pray it must also be a romance with God or your Good. Praise your desire or goal, exalt it, flatter it, kiss it, love it, feel the thrill, and wonder of it all. Let it fire and captivate your imagination. Let it thrill you through and though. Squeeze out the perfume of it. As you meditate on the reality of your desire, feeling the naturalness of the state sought, you are secreting its perfume and entering into the joy of the answered prayer. You are now confirmed in and convinced of this law.

This knowledge is like a sachet of myrrh, cassia, saffron, and cinnamon carried near your heart enabling you to release from the treasure house of eternity the sweet fragrance and perfume of Divinity now and forevermore. It is wonderful.

3

Learn How to Forgive Yourself and Live a Charmed Life

The Sacrament of Penance

The Church says, in speaking of penance, that it is payment made to God for our sins or offences against God. It is taught that confession takes away the guilt of sin and the eternal punishment due to sin, but not the temporal punishment. The purpose of the confession is to forgive sin. The priest says in giving absolution, "I absolve thee from thy sins, in the name of the Father, the Son, and of the Holy Spirit." As a penance, the priest usually instructs the person confessing to repeat certain prayers a certain number of times. These prayers are given as official punishment. It is also taught that sorrow for sins is necessary for confession. In other words, there must be a grief of the soul for having offended God.

If a thing is true, there is a way in which it is true. "The power for forgiving sins," the Roman Catholic Church says, "is based on the statement of Jesus to his disciples. 'Receive ye the Holy Ghost: Whose soever sins ye remit, they are remitted unto them; and whose soever sins ye retain, they are retained.'" JOHN 20:22–23. Let us explain this in simple, everyday language. The word *sin* is from a Greek word meaning to miss the mark. When the Greek archers failed to hit the bull's eye, it was said they sinned or missed the mark. Your goal, desire, objective, or ideal is the mark for which you are aiming. Failure to reach your goal or attain your objective is to sin. You are really sinning when you fail to lead a full and happy life.

A priest in the Bible is one who offers up a sacrifice, namely yourself. You are the priest, and the sacrifice you offer is your desire. You give it up to the subjective mind in the same manner as a farmer gives a seed to the ground. This is why the inner meaning of the word *priest* is subjective mind, intuition, feeling. When you feel that you are what you long to be and you rest in that conviction, you are the priest offering up a sacrifice and forgiving yourself of your sin or your failure to reach the mark.

I want to tell you about a young girl from Nebraska working in an office in Los Angeles. She was shy, timid, hesitant, and felt she was inferior. She had no boy friends. She wanted to be married, have a home of her own, to love and be loved, and to be called Mrs. Jones. I explained to her how to forgive herself for her sin. She was sinning in the true meaning of the word because she failed to realize her desires. Actually by her mental attitude, she was rejecting her good. She began to feel she was wanted, cared for, and admired. She bought a date book in a ten cent store and placed names of admirers in the book. Then she began to imagine she was so popular with men that she could say "no" after looking up the dates in her book. All this was done in her imagination at night and at other times. She became immensely popular with men and was no longer a wallflower. She decided to marry and claimed that Infinite Intelligence attracted to her the ideal companion who harmonized with her perfectly. She imagined the ring on her finger at night as she went to sleep. She would touch and feel the imaginary ring. She actualized the state and fixed it in her consciousness by feeling the naturalness, solidity, and tangibility of the ring; moreover, she said that the ring implied to her that the marriage was already consummated and that she was resting in the accomplished fact. She attracted a most wonderful man, and they blend harmoniously in every way. She forgave herself for her sin.

The word *forgive* means to give for. She gave herself the mood of fulfilled desire for the feeling of lack and limitation. She hit the mark. She realized her goal in life and ceased to sin.

As you read this chapter begin now to realize that you are the priest and that you have the power to forgive yourself of all sins, errors, shortcomings, be they what they may, by putting on the garment or mood of confidence in the law which never fails to respond to your thought and feeling. Let your perception and understanding of the creative law of your own mind be clear, positive, and penetrating. "Whose soever sins ye retain, they are retained." JOHN 20:23.

To retain is to keep, to hold back. If you are poverty-stricken and you join some church, cult, or creed and still remain poor, sick, and needy, you have not forgiven yourself. You are still retaining the mood or belief in poverty and you are not saved. You must demonstrate your savior or your faith in God. We are always demonstrating and manifesting what we believe in.

I visited the Queen of Angels Hospital some time ago to see a man who said he was passing over to the next dimension. The first thing he said to me was, "The Lord Jesus is my savior." Such a statement, of course, is meaningless and makes no sense. The hospitals of the world are full of people who have personal saviors and yet none of them are saved. According to our belief it is done unto us. Our savior is the realization of our desire. Quimby pointed out one hundred years ago that wisdom was our savior and he called this wisdom operating in the mind of man the science of life and of health. Quimby called this Wisdom Christ. *Christ* means your capacity to embrace an idea, induce the mood of it, and weave it into the fabric of your mind through feeling. Your feeling of oneness with your desire is the Spirit of God moving in your behalf which brings your desire to pass; this is the creative law operating in you; such knowledge is your savior as attested to by many who attended two classes on the sacraments given on the West Coast because of their popularity. If you talk to a doctor about your ailment, to a lawyer about a divorce, or a psychologist about your mental troubles, you are confessing or revealing what is bothering you.

A young man attended one of the classes on the sacraments. He had failed in business and lost all the money his parents had given him to open up a store plus all the money they loaned him to pay bills. He was feeling sorry for himself and for his parents. He was also condemning himself which is one of the most destructive of all human emotions. Never condemn yourself or accuse yourself—it is highly destructive. Your mental attitude sends psychic pus throughout your entire system debilitating the entire organism, making you a physical and mental wreck.

The word *repent* means to think in a new way. It means to change your thought and keep it changed. To *forgive yourself* means to identify yourself with your ideal. This young man listened carefully and said to himself, "I can use that teaching." Furthermore, it made sense to him. He began to realize that all he had to do was to dwell on the idea of success and as he did the subjective power would compel him to do all things necessary to be a success. He began to think about success prior to sleep each night. He would think what success meant to him, and how God was always successful in all His undertakings whether planet, sun, or cosmos. He began to realize he was born to succeed and that success meant that he was getting results in his prayer life, that he was successful in his relationship with others, and in his chosen field of expression. He took the idea, "Success is mine now" and repeated it slowly to himself for five or ten minutes every night before he went to sleep. "In the sleepy state," Baudoin, the great psychologist said, "the mind is more receptive and passive, and it is easier to impregnate the subconscious at that time." The sequel is interesting. This young man had an overpowering urge to take up public speaking, which he did. Next, he went to night school and learned about advertising. Today he is a very successful advertising executive with a salary of $25,000.00 a year. When he attended the class on the sacraments, he was getting $50.00 a week plus a few dollars allowance for his car. He confessed his sins and repented in the true meaning of the word. How utterly simple these truths are.

"That ye may know that the Son of man hath power on earth to forgive sins. Arise, take up thy bed and go unto thine house." MATTHEW 9:6. The *Son of man* means the idea, the desire you wish to manifest, and naturally its realization would be forgiveness of your sin (failure to achieve). If in prison, freedom would be forgiveness of your sins. Your sin would be to remain in prison because you desire freedom. By living in the consciousness of freedom you could not stay behind bars. The Angel of God's Presence would open the door of the prison for you. *This angel* would be none other than your conviction of the Power of God to do all things. This is the same angel (mental attitude) which delivered Paul, Peter, and others from prison.

"Take up your bed and walk" is an idiomatic, oriental, graphic way of saying, "Take up the Truth. Rise in consciousness and know that with God all things are possible." Take up the Truth of your own being now and walk the earth a free being. The Truth which sets you free is always the subjective factor; this is the truth behind all things. Whatever you subjectively feel and believe as true comes to pass whether good, bad, or indifferent. Surely this is simple.

If, for example, you say to me like a man did in a recent conversation in Calcutta, "If you want to be holy, you must lead an ascetic life and eat vegetables."

I replied, "That is utter nonsense, but if you believe it, you have made a law unto yourself and you are bound by that law." "Furthermore," I said to him, "God doesn't care whether you eat carrots, peanuts, or wild honey; neither does God care whether you marry or not."

"For John came neither eating nor drinking, and they say, He hath a devil. The Son of man came eating and drinking, and they say, Behold a man gluttonous, and a wine-bibber, a friend of publicans and sinners. But wisdom is justified of her children." MATTHEW 11:18–19. Jesus is telling you in plain language that Wisdom and Divine Understanding consist neither in eating meat nor drinking coffee, nor yet in abstaining from eating and drinking. You can lead an abstemious and ascetic life and be wise, or you can be married and the father of ten children, eat ham and drink coffee, and still be illumined and very wise in the ways of God. Wisdom is independent of either meat or vegetables. Wisdom and the Eternal Verities are always true. If you are a child of wisdom, you will look within and not without for the cause of all and for the source of power. The above mentioned Indian believed there was a great virtue in living apart from the world and eating nuts, fruits, etc.; that is the way it appeared to him. Many others reject that idea as ridiculous and they live among men, enjoy all the good things God provides—good food, God's sunshine, and His flowers. They lead a life of abundance and inner tranquillity; feast on God and all things good. They are full of laughter knowing God doesn't want them to live in a hovel so they live in a beautiful home wearing beautiful and expensive cloths, dressing for God outwardly as well as inwardly leading a balanced life. They fly through the air with the greatest of ease, realizing the plane is God's idea also believing all things are good and very good. These people are illumined, and full of God's Wisdom, and find no virtue in fasting and starving themselves with orange juice and peanuts.

Wisdom knows no sinner or saint. It knows Itself. Why be concerned with non-essentials, with trivial things? Why strain at gnats and at the same time swallow camels—mountains of ignorance, fear, and superstition? It is said by some that God gave power to forgive sins to his disciples and those who followed them by these words, "And I will give thee the keys of the Kingdom of Heaven and whatever thou shalt bind on earth shall be bound in heaven and whatever

thou shalt loose on earth shall be loosed in heaven."
These words *heaven* and *earth* represent the invisible and visible state—your mind and body. The word *body* not only represents your physical body, but your environment, and all things that appertain to your world.

You have the keys to this inner kingdom. You are told over and over again, the Kingdom of Heaven is within. The word *within* means your thought and feeling. The kingdom of infinite intelligence, power, love, bliss, and all of God's riches are in your unconscious depths awaiting resurrection by you. Whatever you bind on earth, or stating it in another way, whatever you believe as true based on sense evidence and appearances, is accepted as true in your consciousness (heaven) and whatever you loose on earth is loosed also in heaven. This means whatever you reject mentally as unfit for mental consumption, whatever you detach your consciousness from and refuse to give attention to, fades out of your life. The reason for lack or limitation in your life is due to the fact you keep these states alive in your consciousness. When we starve the condition to death by rejecting the condition mentally, it dies for want of mental food.

It is not enough to reject the negative condition mentally, we must at the same time feast mentally on our good until we are absorbed in its reality. Then we have loosed the negative state on earth because we loosed it in consciousness or the heavens of our own mind.

The subject of penance and repentance confuses many. "Bring forth therefore fruits meet for repentance." MATTHEW 3:8. To *repent* means, as we previously said, to think in a new way; as you do this, you will bring forth fruit, such as health, happiness, and peace of mind. Many people have rather strange, weird ideas about God, thinking God punishes people for their sins. They have a God of rewards and punishment.

When I was a boy, I used to hear my uncles and aunts conversing about many things; often times they would say, "You know John or Mary met with that accident because he or she ceased going to church." Whenever any calamity came to people, somehow they were considered sinful and the object of the wrath or will of God. I often wondered what kind of a God they had in their mind. What is your concept of God? Don't you know the answer you give to that question determines your whole future? If you think God is cruel, vindictive, an inscrutable tyrannical, cannibalistic Moloch in the skies, a sort of oriental sultan, or despot punishing you, of course, you will experience the result of your habitual thinking and your life will be hazy, confused, and full of fear and limitations of all kinds. In other words, you are expressing the result of your belief about God. You are actually having negative experiences because of your belief. God becomes to you whatever you conceive God to be. Above all things get the right concept of God. It makes no difference what you call God. Your belief or conviction about God governs your whole life.

If, for example, you believe in a God which sends sickness, pain, and suffering, you really believe in a cruel God. You do not have a good God. To you, God is not a loving God. Having such a weird, ignorant concept of God, you experience the result of such a belief in the form of all kinds of difficulties and troubles. Your nominal belief about God is meaningless. The thing that matters is your real, subjective belief— the belief of your heart. You will always demonstrate your belief; that is why Quimby said, "Man is belief expressed."

If you conceive of a God afar off in the skies you will certainly have a God of caprice possessing all the whims of a human being. With such a concept you will be like the business man who said to the writer, "I would be all right if God would leave me alone." Why not go back to the concept of *Isaiah,* chapter 9, verse 6, "His name shall be called Wonderful, Counsellor, the Mighty God, The everlasting Father, The Prince of Peace." Begin now, today, as you read these lines to enthrone the above true concept or belief about God, and miracles will begin to happen in your life. Realize and know that God is all Bliss, all Joy, Indescribable Beauty, Absolute Harmony, Infinite Intelligence, Boundless Love, Omnipotent, Supreme, and the Only Presence. Accept mentally that God is all these things as unhesitatingly as you accept the fact you are alive; then you will begin to experience in your life, the wonderful results of your new convictions about the blessed God within you. You will find your health, your vitality, your business, your environment, and the world in general all changing for the better. You will begin to prosper spiritually, mentally, and materially. Your understanding and spiritual insight will grow in a wonderful way and you will find yourself transformed into a new man.

This is what repentance really means, turning back to the One, the Beautiful, and the Good, counting nothing worthy but your devotion and attention to the One True God, the "Father of lights in whom there is no variableness or shadow of turning."

I have made a study of the work of Philo Judaeus in the First Century dealing with the allegorical exposition of the five books of Moses called the Pentateuch. Philo explains the terms Lord and Lord God in a wonderful way. You have seen these terms frequently in the Bible. Philo says, "The Name denoting the Kind and Gracious Power is God and that denoting the kingly ruling power is Lord." The prayer worthy of the highest admiration in the light of Philo is that one in which the Lord becomes to you God, and you cease to express any fear of Him, but lovingly give honor to Him as the Bestower of all kindness. The words *Lord* and *God* are used interchangeably also. The psalmist says "Know ye that the Lord he is God." Psalms 100:3.

It depends how man looks at God whether he calls on Lord or God. These are simply two ways of looking at the same thing. Lord is the name for the Kingly Ruling Power as Philo says, but in ancient times the term Lord was given also to tyrants, despots, and others who had people under them serving as slaves and serfs. The condition was somewhat like the condition of slaves in the United States before their emancipation. The owner was their lord and master, and they were completely at his mercy. This is the way many people look upon God. They have a cruel, vengeful God. He is a cruel Lord causing earthquakes, disasters of all kinds called "acts of God" in insurance policies. They say, "It is God's will my child died," or if someone says the child was born dead, they say "It is God's will." What a frightful, monstrous concept of God. Philo would have you look upon God as Love; regard It as your Great Benefactor.

I told one of our students in London, England, where I give a class almost every year, to look upon God as his Silent Partner, his Guide, his Comforter, to believe that God was always watching over him like a Loving Father, and to claim that God was always supplying his needs, inspiring him in all his ways. He wrote me saying, "I feel God is a Living Presence, a Friend, a Counselor, a Guide. My business has prospered three hundred per cent, my health has been restored, and I have thrown away the thick lenses I wore for twenty years."

You can see what happened. He looked upon God as his Father. The word *father* meant something to him. It meant love, protection, guidance, and supply. God to him was a person. Troward would say, "There is a way in which that is true." God is Timeless, Shapeless, Ageless, without face, form, or figure. God is the Living Spirit Almighty—personal in the sense that all the elements of personality are in God and are reflected in us, such as life, love, truth, beauty, joy, kindness, and gentleness. The gladness and warmth of your personality is revealing the Infinite Personality of God. God is Law, but God is more than law. God is Love, Light, Truth, Beauty, Wisdom, Joy, Order, Symmetry, Proportion, Rhythm, and Divine Order. God is Laughter, also, and the smile of a child is the smile of God.

What kind of a God do you have? To think of God, therefore, as your Heavenly Father full of Love, Light, and Beauty, and to realize that God is the Infinite Intelligence within whose Nature is Responsiveness causes you to get an immediate response according to the nature of your thought. You experience the reaction as inspiration, guidance, vitality, enthusiasm, prosperity, and other countless blessings. If your thoughts are negative all day long, to use Troward's phraseology, you place yourself in the position of inverting the use of the Power and It flows to you as negative experiences, such as lack, want, misery, pain, and suffering.

In order for man to awaken to freedom and peace of mind, he must certainly repent in the true sense of the term; i.e., he must realize that his experiences are the result of his habitual thinking. He is then discovering the Truth which can set him free.

I was asked this question in our class on the sacraments. "Why were the forty-four people blown up in the plane by the bomb over Denver?" These questions have always been asked. I like the answer Dr. Nicoll gives to that question in his writings. He cites the story in the Bible where the disciples asked Jesus the same question. "There were present, at that season, some that told him of the Galilaeans whose blood Pilate had mingled with their sacrifices. And Jesus answering said unto them, "Suppose ye that these Galilae-ans were sinners above all the Galilaeans, because they suffered such things? I tell you Nay: but, except ye repent ye shall all likewise perish. Of those eigh-teen, upon whom the tower in Siloam fell, and slew them, think ye that they were sinners above all men that dwelt in Jerusalem? I tell you, Nay: but, except ye repent, ye shall all likewise perish." LUKE 13:1–5.

You will see by the above that the disciples were under that age-old, superstitious belief that an angry God had punished these men because the tower fell on them; that somehow it was in punishment for their sins; or others today might say, it was their *karma*, which is another word for belief in a devil, only they have modernized it and called it *karma*. The lat-ter word means law of action and reaction. Action is thought. Reaction is response to your thought. It means sowing and reaping, mentally speaking. The person who asked the question about the forty-four passengers on the plane said, "It must have been their *karma*."

The answer to the question is the same as Jesus gave, "Except ye repent, ye shall all likewise perish."

I knew a student who had planned to go on that flight from the east. She told me that she always prays for guidance and Divine right action claiming, "And the Lord, He it is that doth go before thee." A friend insisted that she drive with her to Los Angeles as she wanted company, so she traveled by car; moreover, she felt intuitively she shouldn't go by plane. It was, she said, as if an inner voice was saying "No," and when the offer came to go by car, she knew she was right. She had been doing her penance or practicing repentance—another name for right thinking—and the wisdom within responded as right action, blessing her in all her ways. Had she not been a praying girl, she would undoubtedly have gone on that ill-fated plane and have been a victim with all the others.

It does not mean, as Jesus pointed out, that these people were bad people. No, not at all; they were victims of the race mind. All of us are immersed in the race mind or the collective unconsciousness which believes in death, accident, misfortune, trouble, and disasters of all kinds. All of us, as Troward says, are subject to the law of averages or race mind until we decide to rise above it through prayer and constructive thinking. The death of hundreds of children in a fire, or young officers blown up in the sea, or drowned in a submarine collision—these experiences have nothing to do with Divine punishment for sins, but they are due rather to the fact that people are immersed in the race mind which is forever conditioning their minds inasmuch as we are all broadcasting and receiving stations.

Quimby says, "Our minds mingle like atmospheres and each has his identity in that atmosphere." The thoughts, feelings, and beliefs induced by news, propaganda, television programs, commentators, plus the mental atmosphere of all those around you are forever impinging on the receptive medium of your mind; unless you do your own thinking, you will, as Jesus says, suffer a common fate; i.e., experiences of people governed by race mind.

Dr. Nicoll points out with radiant lucidity that repentance comes from the Greek *meta-noia* which means change of mind, mental transformation. This word has nothing to do with feeling sorry; neither has it anything to do with the sense of regret. What we need, therefore, is a complete mental housecleaning resulting in a completely new interpretation of life, a new way of thinking, so that we begin now to fill our mind with the Truths of God, thereby crowding out of the mind everything unlike God.

A Japanese Truth student told me during my recent lecture series in Japan that one day he had missed his train because his watch had stopped. He was disappointed for a moment; then he reminded himself that God was always watching over him on his journeys and in all his ways. He learned during the course of the day that the particular train which he had missed had fallen from a cliff, and a great number had been killed and wounded. He added the explanation that when a student contemplates the Presence of God working in him, through him, and around him at all times, and makes a habit of this prayer, the mental and spiritual vibration of that student does not harmonize with the mental vibration of the train that crashes. This is an excellent, scientific explanation based on the law "two unlike things repel each other."

You and I know many good, kind, generous, church-going people who have suffered great tragedies in their lives, not because they are evil, nor because they are thinking about disaster or calamity, but rather because they fail to repent or truly think. How many people think? Thinking means comparing; i.e., comparing one thing with another, one proposition with another; it is your capacity to choose, to select. If the mental instrument can say only "Yes," comparison is not possible. You have a choice between two things—to one you say, "Yes," to the other, "No." All thinking involves, or should involve, selecting this and rejecting that; it would be impossible to select or reject unless your mind had the power of affirmation and rejection. You will see from this that most people do not repent (think wisely). As a matter of fact, what the average person calls thinking is not thinking at all, it is the collective unconscious of the race thinking through him.

You are thinking when your mind is dedicated to the Eternal Truths of God, when you reject all fear and contemplate the reality of your desire, knowing there is an Almighty Power which responds to your thinking and will bring it to pass. You are truly thinking when you reason things out in your own mind, rejecting all negative concepts as unfit for the house of God and feasting on the reality of the Divine solution, knowing that a subjective wisdom responds to your creative thought. You are truly thinking when meditating on whatsoever things are Lovely, Noble, and Godlike. How many do you think are thinking in a new way? They may be good from a worldly standpoint like the men on whom the tower of Siloam fell, but they are not thinking of God and His laws.

It is written, "Thou shalt worship the Lord the God and Him only shalt thou serve." Many good people, good in the sense that they are kind, say their prayers, are good citizens, pay their taxes, and vote every year, but that is not enough. If you looked inside their consciousness, you might find fear, phobias, fixations, grudges, ill will, suppressed resentment, and hate. I talk to many good people in the way the world means it and I find some are afraid of punishment in after life. They still distrust God since they are doubtful of His Love and Grace.

Troward gives the answer to the whole thing when he points out that this law of averages governs man in such a way that large numbers of individuals live and die, but the race or type is always preserved. "So careful of the type it seems so careless of the single life." He points out that you come out of this law of averages or race mind which believes in death, misfortune, sickness, failure, etc., by rising on the scale of intelligence. In other words as you become consciously aware of the fact that the spirit within you is God which responds to your thought, you rise above the law of averages and you no longer are subject to the world-mind and its false beliefs. You begin to take charge of your own life through constructive thoughts and Divine imagery causing a tremendous increase of freedom and sense of security to take place in your life which is always commensurate with the degree of your intelligence or spiritual awareness.

The difference between the man who repents and the man who just sits and lets the world go by saying, "I'm all right, I eat, sleep, and work, and God is good to me" is this: One is thinking wisely, and the Principle of Intelligence reacts accordingly by extending the border of his tent and increasing his freedom along all lines. The other man who just sleeps and eats is simply refusing to use the God-given Power within to rise above the world and its fears; he finds himself getting the flu when it comes around, or hay fever when timothy grass appears. He is open to the aches, pains, and confusion of the world. He remains governed by sense-evidence and race-belief, and lives under the law of averages.

I spoke to a woman one time in the Post Graduate Hospital in New York. She had cancer. She confessed to me that she had hated her daughter-in-law like poison for thirty years, to use her own expression. She said she never thought of cancer or feared it, all of which was true, but the destructive, poisonous emotion lodged in her subconscious and took the form of cancer in her body. You don't have to think or fear cancer to get it; neither do you have to hate anyone in order to have it.

I recently spent some time with a very kind man—noble, generous, and magnanimous in every way. He had cancer all over his body; the reason was his father and two brothers died from it. He feared he would get it. He said he had lived with that terrible fear for over twenty years, "What I fear most has come upon me." It was not God punishing him; neither was it some past *karma* but it was all due to ignorance and fear on his part. No one ever told him how to pray. When he did pray, he was begging some far off God saying, "If it is God's will, he will heal me." Here again you see the old jungle God, an avenging God punishing his children. This man, having now a new concept of God, is well on the way to recovery, receiving encouragement and praise from his physicians.

Most people, when they read about train accidents, auto disasters, etc., seem to think that some outside force comes from somewhere and does harm to people who are entirely innocent; but the mental state and the disasters are "birds of a feather" and "flock together." A man with a strong faith trusting that an Overshadowing Providence is always watching over him is kept away from an unpleasant experience that might hurt or injure him in some way in the same way that oil and water repel each other. The man's faith in God and the unpleasant experience repel each other according to the law of belief.

Say now, to yourself, "I dwell in the secret place of the most High and shall abide under the shadow of the Almighty." Psalms 91:1. If you believe this in your heart, you positively will be invulnerable against all misfortune. You will have nothing at all to fear in this world. There is a mental attitude and a mental cause behind all accidents, fires, wars, and calamities of all kinds. Man is cause and also effect. You might be asking now, "What about natural calamity? can we be protected from that?" We must remember man's environment is always a shadow or reflection of his own mind. If his mind is turned toward God and His Love, he will never be hurt or burned by any calamity, flood, war, or earthquake.

Dr. Taniguchi, leader of New Thought in Japan, and called the Ghandi of that country, points out that a flood in one of the towns in Japan wiped out a number of restaurants, leaving no trace behind. The restaurant, Hiragi-Ya at Yase, which was a meeting place for Japanese Truth students, was intact. Misfortune or calamity of any kind cannot be experienced by the person who believes that God's Truth is his shield and buckler. I believe wholeheartedly what Dr. Taniguchi says, "Heavy rain, windstorm, and earthquake are all productions of the mind."

I am frequently asked that age-old question, "What about children? They are innocent. A man of eighty or ninety is as much of a child as the child in the cradle. There is only one law and it is no respecter of persons. All children are born in the race mind, and, as Quimby points out, they are completely subject to the mental atmosphere of the home where they grow up in the image and likeness of the dominant mental moods of the parents and those around them. If mother gets terribly excited, the little child gets fever, etc., in the same manner that the girl in the office gets a cold because she sits near a fan in the office.

The man of seventy-five, crippled with arthritis, is like the little child crying in the wilderness saying,

"How did this happen to me?" He blames the weather, diet, or something else. He would never think of blaming himself, his thought, or lack of thought. All people in the world are, like children in the cradle, governed by a race mind until they come to the use of reason and begin to think God's thoughts of peace, joy, health, and love.

When we begin to claim what is true of God is true of us, we are coming out from among them (race mind) and we are separate (taking charge of our own destiny). Parents are to do the thinking for children until they learn to reject the unsavory food of false belief, ignorance, and superstition. Ignorance is really the only sin in the universe, and the only punishment is the inevitable consequence of such ignorance. "Repent for the kingdom of Heaven is at hand." Turn to God now by a process of thought and you will find God is your own consciousness; this is your salvation. The word *salvation* means *soteria*—a safe return; that is all it means. How simple, how beautiful that word is! No matter who you are; no matter what crime you may have committed, there is only soteria for you. Yes, a safe return back to the father like the return of the prodigal son. Beggar, thief, and holy man, all shall see the Transcendent Glory which God is; this is the ultimate destiny of all men. God couldn't have it any other way for God is Love.

Turn to God now and feel the truth of the words, "Thou art my hiding place; thou shalt preserve me from trouble; thou shalt compass me about with songs of deliverance." Psalms 32:7. Repent now by changing your thoughts; keep them changed, and the universal heart of God will pour out His blessings on you. You will then sing with the psalmist, "God is our refuge and strength, a very present help in trouble." Psalms 46:1.

4

Wonders Happen When You Pray

Eucharist—Holy Communion

The cause of sickness, lack, and limitation is due to the fact man has surrendered his real heritage (spiritual dominion). Man's free will ends when he makes the wrong choice—a belief and faith in outer effects; this is really the meaning of the fall of man, the original sin. Man has forgotten his Divine Source and has made the opinions of man the Commandments of God. The problem of salvation is getting back to the choice of good—our Father's Kingdom within. The sense of separation from the One God is original sin (falling away from or missing the mark). We are then the fallen angel, i.e., fallen from Heaven, the ideal state. The fall always occurs when a sense of want and deprivation is experienced; this sense of want or lack becomes an urge to growth—to return to The One.

The birth of Christ or Holy Communion is a perpetual process which is experienced whenever you make a better conclusion by arriving at a conviction to be passed on for planting in the subconscious—the strong arm of the One Power. Be careful to make the right choice based on spiritual standards. Never fall into temptation by choosing a false basis of fear-laden beliefs and shallow opinions nourished by propaganda. The sin against the Holy Ghost or the Holy Spirit indicates failure to believe in the One Power ascribing power to outer things, and living in bondage to false gods.

The sacrament of the Eucharist together with all the other sacraments are steps in spiritual rebirth or various stages back to the Father's House; this whole process is known as redemption. The beauty, the glory, the ecstasy, Divine joy, and mystic significance of this process is sometimes lost in the beautiful ceremony and ritual unless we understand the inner meaning of the ritual or dogma. Look at all sacraments as a sacred covenant or agreement between your conscious and subconscious mind. When the two touch and agree on anything, such as health, peace, abundance, or the solution to your problem, God or Peace comes in and steals over your mind.

In sacrifice and sacrament is the basic idea of giving something up to God (your higher self). Since God is all and possesses all already, why give him lambs, bullocks, children, daughters, sons, etc., as if he needed something. We have covered this adequately in the first chapter. We will stress the following point again; however you cannot give God anything but recognition, praise, and thanksgiving. You offer a sacrifice when you give up all your false beliefs and erroneous concepts. Study the proper interpretation of the various sacraments and you will become sanctified (made whole, an integrated personality) by means of your Godlike ideas concerning yourself, your neighbor, your so-called enemies, your relatives, and your God. At the point of conviction, the ideas you entertain will become manifest, for the "word (idea, thought and feeling) is made flesh" according to the sacramental esoteric covenant for "as ye sow, ye shall reap," "for as a man thinketh in his heart (subconscious mind) so is he."

The psychological law behind all this jargon is that the ideas you value or fear the most must objectify sooner or later. In order to practice having Holy Communion daily (communing mentally with wholesome ideas) be sure to train your conscious mind to accept only true and holy concepts concerning man, God, and the cosmos, so that you can do better work and carry on His Holy Will. God's Will for you is always something transcending your wildest dreams. The sacraments teach that your mission is to disclose the hereness, nowness, and isness of God. Man is actually God expressed or made manifest. When you begin to receive Holy Communion which is to silently commune or meditate on the qualities and attributes of God, you will find yourself married to God and all the mysteries of the Heavenly state will begin to unfold to you. God will then work His Holy Will (Whole Will, Life, Love, Truth, Beauty, Order, Bliss, Joy, Abundance, etc.) through you, His beloved son in whom He is well pleased. There must be a merging of yourself with the qualities of God—Truth, Love, Joy—The Only One.

To partake of the sacrament of Holy Communion, man ceases to become a noun and becomes a verb expressing the activity of God. This is the very basis of all sacred theurgical science. *Theos* (God) plus *ergos* (working) equals *theurgy,* or God working which results in healing. When you begin to receive Holy Communion regularly (psychologically speaking), you will never limit the Holy One and you will cease setting up any human beliefs as a barrier. Your awareness or consciousness moves under its own power. Sacr, the root of sacrament, has a phallic connotation, since the sex-power moves under its own power carrying the seeds of life and germination.

The outward receiving of sacraments must be accompanied by the inward growth of grace; unless the outer act is accompanied by an inner change of the heart, nothing is accomplished. The grace you receive becomes an everdawning sense of wonderment that you and God are an organic and functional unit. If you are a practitioner or teacher, you live by grace which means the love and wisdom of God flood your mind and heart; then you speak your word with authority. The teacher, working under grace when he prays for someone, reveals that person as he really is, free from the shackles of wrong beliefs, and sees him with the true Vision of God who pronounces all things good. This is the winning of the crown of glory and grace for your work now. It is written not by might (physical effort), not by power (mental, as in mesmerism), but by the Spirit. As you contemplate the harmony, beauty, and perfection of God for your client, he is freed from *karma* (negative state in subconscious mind) and lives under grace (love) and truth (freedom).

Behind all symbolism, ritual, liturgy, and ceremony you *must* find the inner, ignition spark. The Bible is full of phallic symbolisms, such as found in the Psalms, etc.—Gates—King of Glory—Lord of Hosts, Jonah (idea), and the whale (womb, subconscious mind). All the involved symbology of the sacrament will not mean anything to you unless you understand better the interplay of the conscious mind (Jonah, phallus, King) and the subconscious sometimes called circle, whale, womb, Queen Esther, the Christ within, and the gates of the temple.

Every sacrament is an act of Divine union resulting in a deeper experience of a downpour of grace which is a sense of deep conviction beyond words. Prayer, the ancients knew, was the act of Adam drawing Eve out of his rib, or, to state it in another way, was to draw out the feeling, the mood from the depth of yourself which is appropriate or fit for the beloved desire or ideal. Every man is the fit bridegroom as he comes bearing proper seed concepts worthy of a son of God. When fear, ignorance, and superstition depart from your consciousness, it is a sign that you are really partaking of the various sacraments and entering into a state of grace and spiritual conviction. You know well whereof you speak and send forth your decrees like a king with power from on High.

There is always room at the top in all walks of life; the same is true in this teaching. We have a multitude of workers toiling at valley-level. There is virgin ground on the spiritual level of consciousness.

Quimby took on all challenges, sickness, and lacks of all kinds. He was able to stop in its tracks the thing which his quaking patients feared would come upon them. He introduced in the field of consciousness man operating from an exalted, Godlike state of consciousness. He was full of grace (wisdom and love) and understanding. His exalted mood brought about an electronic induction of grace and confidence in his patients who reported blessings, healings, and gifts divine from the One Source. The vibrations of fear could not and did not persist in the mental atmosphere of such a worker. Quimby discovered what everyone should know that the sign of demonstration or an answer to your prayer occurs when you sense a feeling of rest from striving, a feeling that after all you no longer want it, since subjectively it is done. There is a let down because the creative act has been accomplished. It is finished. Real healing is a matter of basic understanding. Your desire or concept, whatever it is, leave to God to give the increase, to transform your body, and heal an organ for you.

A boy said to me one time when I was teaching a class in catechism, "Bread always remains bread; how can it be changed into something else?" I am sure that all reading these words know a little bit about chemistry. The writer of this book has done research work in the field of Chemistry and Pharmacology. Bread, butter, and milk are changed into blood, flesh, bone, and muscle. The wine and the bread which the Italian and French have for lunch are changed into flesh and blood by the Chemist within. The important part from the standpoint of the Eucharist is the psychological transformation: *Transformation* means the changing from one thing to another. A chemist, through the process of fractional distillation, makes alcohol from sugar or grain. Alcohol can be changed into vinegar by certain ferments. Radium transforms itself into lead. When the ancient alchemists spoke of transforming lead into gold, they had in mind the sublimation of the grosser passions of man into spiritual channels. The purpose of the alchemist was to give birth to a new man by a new way of thinking. The language of alchemy was a secret language like the language of the Bible which is written largely in the language of parable and allegory.

The average man was referred to as lead, and to change lead into gold (spiritual powers) was the object of the alchemist. God represents the Hidden Mine or the Kingdom of Heaven within man. By following the alchemical formulas which were really forms of prayer, the man of lead resurrected the latent God-Powers and became a man of gold. A plant, by a process of photosynthesis transforms the air, water, chemicals, and enzymes of the earth into new substances called nuts, fruits, peas, etc. Let us see how you transform the various and sundry impressions, thoughts, and concepts coming to your mind all day long. Suppose someone calls you a skunk. Do you take Holy Communion, or do you become negative, resentful, and angry? Why should you? Are you a skunk? Why should you permit another to disturb you? Why don't you transform that impression into a Godlike idea by realizing that God's peace floods the mind and heart of the person who said it; this is called transforming impressions. You are digesting and absorbing Truths of God. If you want to partake of the sacrament of Eucharist, you must transform all impressions of life which come to you and make sure only that which is elevating, pleasing, and dignifying is implanted in your mind for digestive purposes. You must change your reactions to life; eating of a wafer or drinking of wine or grape juice won't change you internally. If your reactions to life are mostly negative, you are separated from God and all things good. You are not in tune with the Infinite, neither are you mentally communing with the Holy One, God (Holy Communion).

It is no use to say Mary or John is to blame because he or she does this or talks like that. The point that matters is that you have permitted *yourself* to get negative. You have allowed a gangster and assassin to enter the invisible place, the Secret Place of the Most High. You live in your inner, invisible world of the mind. Look around you now—you see a chair, table, television set perhaps, and the other furniture of the room where you are. Are not your thoughts, feelings, emotions, fears, doubts, and hopes just as real as the furniture? If you allow yourself to identify with any negative emotion, you have eaten unsavory food. You must go back to Holy Communion, mentally engage your thought on the Eternal Verities, and go up the Hill of God by elevating your thought life.

Holy Communion should be a constant practice whereby you look upon God as your Silent Partner and look to Him for strength, sustenance, and guidance. Prayer should be a habit, and you keep prayed up when you constantly think, speak, and act from the standpoint of the Golden Rule.

Here is a test to see if you have really partaken of this sacrament in its spiritual significance. Have you ceased saying "I" to negative thoughts, moods, feelings, impulses, to every feeling of anger, envy, and dislike? Do you say, "I don't like her, I resent him, I am depressed, I hate her, I fear?" When you attach something constructive to "I am" or "I" you are really eating of the bread of Heaven. You create whatever you attach to "I am." If you say, "I hate" or "I resent," you are identified with a negative, destructive emotion and mentally eating unsavory food which will poison you mentally and physically. When walking down the street, you would not enter into a pool of muddy water. In the same manner when you travel psychologically the streets of your mind, you avoid the slums and association with gangsters, murderers, and assassins in your mind, such as fear, ill will, resentment. You can refuse to go along with negative emotions. Avoid them like you would the dark alleys of your city. Your mother told you when you were young to keep away from bad company. Keep away now from bad company in your mind. Do not let negative emotions touch you; neither do you touch them. Begin to realize that the trouble is within you; then you will cease blaming others.

You have heard the story about the Irishman who was shortsighted and refused to wear glasses. He kept saying his eyes were perfect, but he was constantly complaining about the papers, saying they were so badly printed. What thought comes to you when someone criticizes you and spreads lies about you? Observe your reaction, notice it, taste it. Is it pleasant? If you have advanced to the grade of the sacrament of the Eucharist, you will remain unmoved and undisturbed. Your food will be the bread of peace, love, and good will—this is the bread of the silence. You have arrived at that state of consciousness where you know the other can't hurt or disturb you; no one but you can. You refuse, therefore, to eat of negation. You will be full of compassion for the other person; in your understanding you will pray for that person's peace and illumination. Have you had your Holy Communion yet? Do you now see? Do you hear? Do you understand?

The terms *Eucharist, Viaticum, Lord's Supper, Holy Communion, passover* all mean the same thing.

The Synoptic Gospels (Mark 14:22, Matthew 26:26, Luke 22:17) refer to the Last Supper; likewise Paul in I Corinthians 11:23. In ancient times at Jewish meals the following blessing was said over the bread and wine, "Blessed art thou, O Lord our God, King of the Universe, who bringest forth bread from the earth," and before drinking wine, "Blessed art thou who createst the fruit of the vine." The Eucharist, i.e., the ceremony and ritual, had in its earliest form an element in common with the ordinary Jewish meal which was sanctified by thanksgiving uttered over the bread and over the cup. "We are one body: for we all partake of the one loaf." I Corinthians 10:17. To Paul the Eucharist meant the Truth of God which was for Jew and Gentile alike. It was a sacrament representing the unity in God of all people. The single loaf broken into fragments and distributed among the faithful was the pledge of their intimate union.

"Jesus took bread, and blessed it, and brake it, and gave it to the disciples, and said, Take, eat; this is my body. And he took the cup, and gave thanks, and gave it to them, saying, Drink ye all of it; For this is my blood of the new testament, which is shed for many for the remission of sins." Matthew 26:26, 27, 28. The *Book of Common Prayer* teaches that all the Sacraments are simply tokens of a Christian and "signs of grace and God's good will." *Bread* and *wine* are symbols of Divine Substance and Divine Life (see *Steps in Prayer* published 1946). Bread and wine are automatically changed by the Intelligence within you into flesh and blood. In ancient, harvest times people gathered together and shared bread with each other and drank wine. It was a form of thanksgiving and gratitude for a wonderful harvest; but it also portrayed love, a union of many hearts. Bread is made up of many grains of wheat which represent a gathered-togetherness of all our thoughts and emotions in the contemplation of God. In making wine we crush and squeeze out the juice of the grape. This means we must go within and press out of our own consciousness the joy of the answered prayer. Wine symbolizes joy. The cup symbolizes the receptive mind which is capable of receiving and accepting the reality of the desire. Drinking of the wine means the happy, joyful state of mind wherein you pour out love and feeling into your desire and contemplate its reality. Bread and wine indicate a wonderful method of prayer. The word *bread* means not only physical food, but also money, clothing, and all things needed in this three-dimensional plane; furthermore, the word *bread* means spiritual food such as thoughts of peace, love, and happiness.

Man may eat of physical bread, but he will hunger again. The bread you give to others and to yourself is the noble, dignified, Godlike state of conscious-

ness. You must select ideas and thoughts which heal,
activate, bless, inspire, and elevate your mind; thus,
you are eating the bread of Heaven, which is peace,
happiness, and freedom. If a man lives to eat, to get
power over others, or merely to accumulate worldly
honor and riches, he will hunger. He must not neglect
spiritual food and nourishment. He may have all the
material wealth he wishes, for wealth is not of itself, a
deterrent to happiness and spiritual growth, and yet
have peace of mind, joy, and happiness. Man cannot
live without love, beauty, and peace. To spend all your
time in the pursuit of worldly things will bring dis-
illusionment, grief, and sorrow. Man becomes cold,
cruel, callous, and indifferent when he separates himself from the heavenly food of love, good will, charity,
kindness, gentleness, and love of beauty. "Man doth
not live by bread alone but by every word that proceedeth out of the mouth of God doth man live."

When the Bible says, "Take ye and eat; this is my
body," we realize at once that this is a figurative statement, and under any circumstances whatever is not
to be taken literally. Troward says, "If a thing is true
there is a way in which it is true." Every formed thing,
whether a solar planet or the desk you are seated at,
represents the body of God. The whole world is really
the body or form of God—God made manifest. Matter is Spirit in form, or Spirit reduced to the point of

visibility. No matter what we eat at the table may be considered the body of God, and whatever we drink, whether milk, coffee, or grape juice, could be called the blood or Life of God. We know, of course, the food we eat is consumed and transformed into energy, new cells, and in general contributes to our well-being.

The Bible is a psychological document and is not referring to material things expect indirectly. It uses outer, concrete things to represent inner psychological states of mind. When it speaks of *body*, it means your pictorial image or ideal. When the ideal or image is impressed on the subconscious, it is made manifest in the exact image and likeness of the mood that entertained it.

For example, if your ideal is to become a great singer, this ideal captivates your mind and generates a delightful mood or feeling; this mood conceals the body or form of your ideal. The mood is the Father which generates its likeness on the objective plane. "As within, so without." (See *Steps in Prayer*, page 22.) The oak is contained in the acorn, so also is the mustard plant in the mustard seed. In other words the body or form of the mustard plant is in the seed already. Jesus said, "Labour not for the meat which perisheth, but for that meat which endureth unto everlasting life." JOHN 6:27. "For the bread of God is he which cometh down from heaven, and giveth life unto the world.

Then said they unto him, Lord, evermore give us this bread. And Jesus said, unto them, I am the bread of life." JOHN 6:33, 34, 35.

By *bread* is meant all that is spiritual, such as faith, hope, trust, and confidence in God which come from the heavens of our mind and give life to our ideas. These moods and feelings are the bread of Heaven. Such mental attitudes overcome appearances of things and all sense-evidence. *Bread* is the inner power which the illumined mind draws from the inexhaustible storehouse within. The spiritual meaning of anything is its real meaning. All physical or external things are but shadows or symbols of spiritual realities. The *Truth* is bread which feeds our soul, refreshes our mind, changes the eater, and is not itself changed into the eater. Referring to the allegorical *manna* or heavenly food, "the bread which the Lord hath given you to eat" EXODUS 16:15. Philo writes, "Dost thou not see the food of the soul, what it is? It is the continuing Logos (Intelligence, Light, Divine Idea) of God, like unto dew, encircling the soul on all sides." "I am the bread of Life." JOHN 6:35. I AM is the name of God, meaning Life, Awareness, the Formless, Faceless Presence within us, The Living Spirit Almighty. I AM is first person, present tense.

Mentally feast on God or the Good now. Feast on your desire and its reality. Continue to eat mentally of your ideal until you reach the point of acceptance or conviction. *Conviction* means that you engage your mind on a certain goal until you reach or get the reaction which satisfies. This is the place of fulfillment. You have eaten fully and all is well. Troward tells you always to go to the end in prayer; having imagined and felt the end, you have willed the means to the realization of the end. If you continue to feast on the accomplished fact, the moment comes when you can eat no more; then you say, "It is finished," or "Amen." These words of confirmation refer to the finished, psychological state of consciousness where you subjectively know that the thing prayed for is a fact in consciousness. You do not have objective proof as yet, but you are not waiting for results because you know the moment you think not, the manifestation or demonstration will appear. You remain unmoved in the absolute conviction that the solution felt as true within must be experienced without.

As you walk the street or drive your car, you may eat the bread of Heaven by sensing and feeling the God-Presence within you. You know this God-Wisdom and Power can overcome, transcend, modify, and transform any obstacle or discordant circumstances in the physical world. You are eating of the bread of Heaven when you know that the internal world of the mind and spirit is causative, and that the subjective always overturns and overthrows the objective. Your constructive consciousness, full of faith and confidence, supplants the mood of fear and lack, and your answer comes.

To certain religious groups the Mass is said to repeat, in an unbloody but true way, the death of Jesus. It is called the sacrifice of the body and blood of Christ, really present on the altar under the appearance of wine and bread. Mass is offered for the living and also the so-called dead. In the Catholic Church it is believed Christ is mystically slain in a way that the human, finite mind cannot understand. The doctrine of transubstantiation, which teaches that the wafer and wine are transformed into the actual flesh and blood of Jesus, cannot be taken as literally true. When the Psalmist sang, "O taste and see that the Lord is good," PSALMS 34:8, he referred to the response man receives when he turns in thought to the Divine Intelligence within him. He feels its response. It is sweet and gives him a sense of pleasure and deep satisfaction. *To taste* is to appropriate. When you eat of an idea mentally, you are tasting its savor and you rejoice in its digestion.

The following verses are always quoted in support of the literal interpretation of flesh and blood. "Whoso eateth my flesh, and drinketh my blood, hath eternal life; and I will raise him up at the last day. For my flesh is meat indeed, and my blood is drink indeed. He that eateth my flesh, and drinketh my blood, dwelleth in me, and I in him." JOHN 6:54, 55, 56. "This is an hard saying; who can hear it?" JOHN 6:60. "From that time many of his disciples went back, and walked no more with him." JOHN 6:66. In verse 63 of JOHN 6, Jesus explains the whole subject for all who have eyes to see and ears to hear. "It is the spirit that quickeneth; the flesh profiteth nothing: the words that I speak unto you, they are spirit, and they are life." In other words, he is talking figuratively and psychologically. The words are spirit—something you feel and sense in your heart, a movement of consciousness. The words are full of life in the sense that the ideas you entertain animate, sustain, inspire, and lift you up. The flesh profiteth nothing. The *flesh* means that the outer ceremony, ritual, formula, and wafer, is meaningless unless accompanied by an interior change. The mechanical repetition of a prayer is also meaningless. Prayer is a movement of consciousness. It is, as Emerson said, "The contemplation of things from the highest standpoint." Socrates gave the answer when he said in Plato's *Phaedrus*, "May the outward and inward man be at one." When Jesus said, "It is the spirit that quickeneth," He is referring to an inner feeling, awareness, an inward sign of grace. By *grace* is meant a deep, inner sense of harmony and love. When the inner harmony reveals outer harmony, you are living in grace. No matter what disturbances or shocks occur at the periphery of our life, if we are truly living in grace, we will go back to the Divine Center within, and there rest in peace and in confidence, gathering strength and power to overcome all obstacles.

One time I knew a man who was a very brilliant chemist. He never did anything but dream about new inventions, new formulas, and new discoveries. He had formulas given to him in a dream which he discarded. He said to me once, "You know, I had a dream last night and I saw a formula explained in detail."

I said to him, "Perhaps that was the answer to your problem of synthesis."

He ridiculed the idea saying, "I said, it was only a dream." He would go three times a week to Holy Communion; after receiving the wafer he would feel very good, happy, and radiant for several hours following until someone criticized his work or something went wrong; then he would go into a tantrum.

I explained to him one day in detail why he felt so good after receiving the Eucharist or wafer. This is the essence of what I said: "You believe that you are actually eating the flesh and blood of Jesus in a wafer; this acts as a powerful auto-suggestion to your subconscious mind, causing it to respond with a sense of well-being, joy, and inner sense of gladness; this new mood of yours is all due to expectancy. You have prepared your mind to receive grace and according to your belief is it done unto you. You are really a slave to a wafer and completely dependent upon it for a sense of peace and security. In other words, you are a victim of suggestion. Supposing you were up front in the battle lines, or the ship or airplane in which you were traveling got into trouble, what would you do? Where would you get the strength, comfort, guidance, and protection you would need at that moment?" Then I explained to him that he could contact God within himself through his own thought and that there would be an immediate response for the nature of Infinite Intelligence, as Troward says, is "responsiveness." He could by meditation, i.e., by mentally absorbing and eating of an idea, induce a mood of peace, confidence, trust, and even ecstasy.

I explained to him about a soldier in the first World War, all alone in a trench, surrounded by the enemy. The soldier recited slowly the words of the Twenty-third Psalm. He drank in each word, believing in his heart that God was his shepherd, watching over him, taking care of him. He trusted this Overshadowing Presence to lead him to safety. A terrific storm arose and the enemy battalion retreated several miles to another location; this young soldier, saved by an inner strength, an inner confidence, walked through the woods twenty miles and found his comrades.

This soldier told me that as he prayed, "God is my shepherd, He leadeth me beside the still waters," a sudden wave of peace and comfort seized his whole being and he was exalted and lifted up spiritually. The soldier had partaken of Holy Communion. He had turned to the God-Power in his thought and had received a transfusion of the Holy Spirit which brought about a strong, calm, mental atmosphere blessing his inner life. He was not dependent on a wafer or wine which remains flour and wine regardless of all the prayers said over it. It is, of course, changed into your body and blood when you eat the wafer and drink the wine and its substance is changed by the Great Chemist within into new cells, nerves, tissues, muscles, and blood. It becomes flesh of your flesh and bone of your bone in a physical sense.

After considerable discussion with my chemist friend along these lines, he became intensely interested and is now teaching others about the Hidden Power.

Eating of the body and drinking of the blood refers purely to psychological transformations and nothing else. What about the impressions that come to you during the day? Begin now the art of transforming them. Are you working on your negative emotions, inner discord, and destructive imagination? The transforming power is at the place of the intake of impressions—your inner mind. Begin to think in a new way and you will become a new man. As long as you think in the same way, nothing changes. To change your life does not mean changing outer circumstances and conditions; it is to change all your mental and emotional reactions to life. Do you always react the same way to people, to news, to conditions? Are you stereotyped in your reactions? Watch your reactions now, today. See if they are mostly negative. If negative, you are not eating of the bread of Heaven because you are not transforming the impressions which come to you. You must never permit news, propaganda, criticism, and statements of others to provoke negative reactions in you. When you are tempted to react negatively, stop immediately and say, "God thinks, speaks, and acts through me"; then a great wave of peace will steal over you; this is the bread of Heaven; eat of it all day long. Return love for hate, peace for pain, good will for envy, and as you continue to do this, an internal peace will prevail, proving the sacramental act, which is your covenant or agreement with the good.

By turning to the Spirit within, we receive nutrition and power; this is the food and bread of the silence, the bread of love and peace. By partaking of this inner, wonderful food, we shall never hunger, neither shall we get faint or weary. Keep on eating the bread of righteousness, which is right thought, right feeling, and right action; this will pay you tremendous dividends.

In the Lord's Prayer we read, "Give us this day our daily bread." MATTHEW 6:11. The Lord's Prayer antedates Christianity and stems from an ancient Jewish prayer called the *Kadish* which indicates that the truth and meaning of bread was universally understood. In looking to God as your Universal Source of supply, knowing that His supply is your supply now, and that there is always a Divine surplus in your life, means that you are claiming your daily bread, which was given to you from the foundation of time. The inner and the outer man is forever fed and nourished by God's Wisdom and Love. The soul of man cries out for Wisdom, Truth, and Beauty, which is the food of the wise. God's ideas are Infinite. You can pass on some of these ideas to others, thereby breaking the bread of God, sharing it with all who hunger. The Christ in you is the true bread of life. Paul says, "The Christ in you, the hope of Glory." Christ is the Presence of God in all men. The feast of bread and wine is called the Last Supper because it is the last psychological feast you partake of before you pass over from pain to peace or from limitation to freedom. The solution to your problem is your savior.

An actress in one of my classes some years ago was unemployed for a long time. I explained Holy Communion to her. She said she received it every week at church but she was still unemployed and obviously in want. She had not discovered her savior. I gave her a new idea which penetrated her mind. "Take ye and eat, this is my body;" she now understood the body to mean that the plant was in the seed; the apple tree was in the seed, the form of expression is also in the desire.

Troward states it beautifully when he says, "The desire (idea) has its own mathematics and mechanics with it. You don't add power to the seed or energy, you place it in the soil and it will grow of its own volition." She ate the body of Christ by accepting the idea of a contract in her mind. The idea is dead and static by itself. We must give life to the idea. We must quicken it. Being an artist, she was quick to see and understand. She knew she had to take the cup and drink the wine or blood, a figurative way of saying she had to call forth the feeling, the enthusiasm or, to quote Troward, "We have to enter into the spirit of it." The *spirit* is always the animation, the movement of consciousness, the warmth, the life of the idea. It is the spirit of the game, the spirit of the artist, the spirit of the musician, the spirit of the man in prayer. She was drinking the wine of life when she was imbibing the reality of the idea and feeling the thrill and wonder of it all. She used to imagine that I was congratulating her on her wonderful contract. She used to do this for three or four minutes two or three times a day. She would hear the voice and feel the thrill. The frequent engagement of her mind on this mental picture (see chapter "Imagination" in my book *Believe in Yourself*) brought an impregnation of the idea in her subconscious and before the class terminated she received a wonderful contract at a fabulous salary.

When Jesus took bread and blessed it, that simply means your idea, your desire, plan, enterprise, your wish, that which you want to be, to do, and to have. The idea or desire is the male element; then you must drink of the cup which is the feeling, the receptive mind which receives. The cup, or heart, is the subjective in man, the seat of emotions and feeling. In other words, thought and feeling, husband and wife, idea and emotion, must blend together and become one; then your prayer is answered. To state it in another way—whenever your conscious and subconscious mind synchronize and unite with any idea or desire—it is established and made manifest. You could explain the drama in many ways; yet it all comes back to a simple, universal process of prayer: It is the feeling, emotional, or subjective nature of man and woman that accepts the idea or desire, giving it form and function.

In some cathedrals you have seen the saint's head on his heart; this symbolizes the union of the mind and heart in all prayer, or in biblical language, the body and the blood of Christ. The word *Christ* means Logos or the I AM, God, the Life Principle in us. In other words, Christ is the way the Life Principle works. You are Christ in one sense when you know that thought and feeling create your destiny; then you have discovered Wisdom. Quimby called Wisdom—Christ. Knowing that thoughts are things and that your feeling nature is the Spirit of God, you can, therefore, transcend all obstacles and deliver yourself from all discouragement, lack, and despair.

When the priest places a quantity of wine in the chalice and adds some water, the act is symbolic of the union of mind and wisdom. The *wine*, rich and strong, represents the qualities, attributes, and potencies of God; the *water* represents the mind always in motion. It is the marriage or union of love and wisdom which brings forth the science of health, happiness, and peace of mind spoken of by Quimby one hundred years ago.

The words of the priest when he distributes Holy Communion are rarely understood in their true significance. "May the Body of our Lord, Jesus Christ preserve thy soul into life everlasting." Interpreted properly, all it means is this: the idea, the knowledge, the awareness that your own I AMNESS is the Lord Jesus Christ, enables you to preserve your soul or subconscious from negative influence as you will no longer attach anything negative to I AM. Jesus means I AM or God within you. Christ means savior. Your I AM or God is your savior. In other words, all it is saying when translated from Hebrew or Greek is to acknowledge the Presence of God within. Accept It, tune in on It, and the Holy Presence will heal, bless, answer your prayer, and solve all your problems, for "with God all things are possible."

As the priest washes his hands during mass he says, "Lord, I have loved the beauty of Thy house and the place where Thy Glory dwelleth." You are the house of God, and the Indescribable Beauty of God indwells you; the Glory, meaning the Infinite Intelligence and Wisdom of God, also dwells within waiting for you to call upon it. You love His Beauty and Glory as you turn to Him in reverence, adoration, and in complete recognition of His Absolute Sovereignty. Looking upon the Spiritual Power as the source of your health, wealth, energy, and all things, you are loving it. All of us are in constant need of Holy Communion, i.e., union with the Spirit within. We need to dedicate our lives and actions to God. Internal strength and faith in God are our greatest defenses against the encroachments of negative thoughts and pressures from the external side of life.

If you want to drink the blood of Christ, if you wish to find the Holy Grail or the Holy Cup, you will find it in your own heart called the Chamber of His Holy Presence. Open your mind and heart now and let in the influx of the Holy Spirit. Go on a great psychological, mystical banquet by meditating on Love, Light, Wisdom, Power, and Peace. You will find your heart (cup) will become filled full of the blood of Christ or the life of the Truths contemplated. "Drink ye all of it." It is the love of God welling up in your heart. Pass this mystic cup to others. You do this by rejoicing in the Love and Beauty of God flowing through all those around you and through all men everywhere. Realize in your heart as you walk the streets, as you enter your own house or office, that all people you meet are partaking of that cup of Love, Light, and Truth. You are now blessing others; praying in that way, you will always abide in the joy of good works. Now you bear witness to the Christ; you testify to the Holy One within because your heart is full of love and good will. Drink every drop of the cup. It is the dew of Heaven, and you find yourself in a state of indescribable bliss. You are dead to the old state and you live in the new.

"This is my blood of the new testament which is shed for many for the remission of sins." MATTHEW 26:28. Having come to this point, you know that in order to really transform yourself or heal another you have to shed your blood; i.e., give life to the idea, activate it, and charge it with interest which is feeling.

Now you are giving your life to the new idea, and the old idea dies because you took your attention from it. You testify to the new state, and your sins are remitted or forgiven. The sin is to miss the mark, the target, or your failure to realize your desire. As long as you desire something, you are sinning because you fail to realize it. As soon as you enter into a realization of complete mental acceptance of your desire, the Savior or Christ is born, and you are at peace; this is called the blood of the new testament meaning you are testifying to a new state.

If your mother is sick, you must shed your blood on a cross for her in order to help her. It is, of course, foolish to take these things literally. The words of the Bible are allegorical, figurative, and psychological. I heard a man in Hyde Park in London in 1921 say something similar to the above. I thought it strange then, but shortly afterwards I knew what he meant. The idea of health is real—it is of God. Therefore, you take your mother's request (her cross); make it your own and go within yourself to God, saying and affirming, "Here in the secret place all is bliss, joy, happiness, perfection, glory, light, and love." As you give life, love, and feeling to the idea of your mother's perfection and as you claim that what is true of God is true of her, you are shedding your blood (giving life to the idea of health, harmony, and peace). You will continue to shed your blood by frequent occupancy of the mind with the prayer until you die to the belief in her sickness and resurrect your conviction of the way it is in God and Heaven. There being but one mind, what you felt as true in that atmosphere of health and peace will be resurrected in her experience. You died in Golgotha (place of imagination and feeling) and shed your blood for your mother and for the remission of her sins. Her sin (sickness) has disappeared and health is resurrected. You experienced the crucifixion (crossing over) or the passover, two words meaning the same thing. You crossed over from the conscious mind, belief in sickness, to the subjective belief in perfect health. You succeeded in conveying the idea of perfect health to the subconscious through repetition, faith, and expectancy; that is the crucifixion.

This should be shouted from the house-tops. We should cease telling people that the Jews killed our savior. We should begin to tell the Truth to all men that man is his own savior for God indwells him. We must cease perpetuating class and religious hatred which will continue as long as we teach the literal meaning of the crucifixion. To read the Bible literally it becomes a monotonous, sadistic document giving the impression that God is a cannibalistic Moloch seeking bloody sacrifices. "Draw out and take you a lamb according to your families, and kill the passover." Exodus 12:21. Here is the same drama as the Eucharist—Lord's Supper or Holy Communion. You draw out a lamb which means your desire comes out of consciousness. You must kill the desire by identifying with it and absorbing its reality like a sponge absorbs water. Your desire is now a living conviction. You spilled the blood of the lamb on your desire. The blood of the lamb is simply your inner mood of faith and confidence in your capacity to impregnate your subconscious with your desire through feeling its reality. You sprinkle the blood on the door of your senses and all the Egyptians (negative thoughts) are destroyed.

Let your five senses become anointed with the wisdom and intelligence of God, and as you awaken to your inner power, you will cast the spell of God around you. Therefore, no evil shall befall you; neither shall any plague come nigh thy dwelling. You are now married to God, i.e., mentally and emotionally united to God and all things good. "Your cup runneth over and goodness and mercy shall follow thee all the days of thy life." Psalms 23:5, 6.

5

Techniques for Spiritual Unfoldment

Holy Orders

Place yourself under holy orders now and miracles will begin to happen in your life. You confer holy orders on yourself when you begin to practice the Presence of God all day long; whenever your attention wanders away, bring it back to the contemplation of His Holy Presence in all things and in all people everywhere. You are now a moving, healing force. You are ordained. You can no longer be fearful or timid for you are under holy orders—orders of the Holy One (God).

It is said by some churches that Jesus instituted holy orders when at the last supper he said to his disciples, "Do this in remembrance of me." LUKE 22:19. "Whose soever sins ye remit, they are remitted unto them; and whose soever sins ye retain, they are retained." JOHN 20:23. "Thou art a priest for ever after the order of Melchizedek." PSALMS 110–4. "Without father, without mother, without descent, having neither beginning of days, nor end of life; but made like unto the Son of God; abideth a priest continually." HEBREWS 7:3.

The word *Melchizedek* is symbolic of the God-self within you. The God-Presence has no father or mother, so it is really simple to realize that you are the priest yourself. You are told in the seventh chapter of *Hebrews* that Melchizedek is King of righteousness, King of Salem, meaning King of peace. You are the high priest, and the offering or sacrifice you make is your desire; i.e., you turn over your ideal to your deeper mind which is the great fabricator that brings it to pass in due season. A priest is a mediator—you are always mediating or bringing about through scientific prayer a Divine adjustment in your mind. As you read these pages, perhaps you are saying to yourself, "I want victory over this difficulty," or perhaps you wish a perfect healing.

One of our radio listeners recently heard me speak about the way a young girl healed herself of cancer. She kept repeating to herself frequently with deep feeling and conviction, "Only God and His love grows in every atom of my being." She filled her mind with that truth and her physician complimented her on her great faith. She was a priest offering up her sacrifice, meaning she turned away from the problem and entered into the feeling or consciousness of health which was her savior or salvation. She mediated between the invisible and the visible. She called on the invisible healing power which responded to her faith and was made visible in her body as perfect health. Her mental attitude of receptivity, acceptance, and faith carried her out of that state of pain and suffering to health and peace of mind.

Perhaps you have certain desires which you have failed to realize. Become now the real priest and resolve the conflict. Your feeling is the priest which enables you to move in consciousness from one state to another. If, for example, you look at your problem now, it has within it the solution or answer in the form of a desire. The realization of your desire would save you. If poor, begin now to feel wealthy. Enter into the spirit of opulence. Imagine and feel you are wealthy and prosperous. As you continue to do this, you are the priest mediating or making peace between that which you now are and that which you want to be. You will discover that the feeling of wealth actually produces wealth. You have given up the mood of poverty for the mood of opulence. You are the king of righteousness, meaning you practice right thought, right feeling, and right action. You are a king because you have complete control of your own realm of the mind. You can order your thoughts around and cause them to obey you instantly. You know that there is always a way out and an answer. When fear, belief in other powers, rumor, propaganda, or scare headlines crowd into your mind with overwhelming force, recall at that moment that you are a priest of God and under holy orders to bring forth harmony, health, and peace. You must remain absolutely faithful and steadfast to your ideal. As you continue to dwell on your goal, you are climbing the hill of God; as you continue to climb mentally, you will enter the fixed or conditioned state of consciousness called answered prayer.

The bishop says to the priest about to be ordained, "Receive power to sacrifice to God and offer mass for the living and the dead in the name of the Lord. Amen." After repeating the Creed, the bishop lays his hand on the head of the priest repeating, "Receive the Holy Ghost whose sins you shall forgive, they are forgiven them and whose sins you shall retain, they are retained." You receive the Holy Ghost when you sense your oneness with God and all things good. Through your knowledge of the laws of mind, you have the power to forgive sins because all you have to do is to identify yourself emotionally with your desire—this is hitting the mark. You have then ceased to sin or miss the mark you are shooting for in life.

I will now interpret the Apostles' Creed for you. It was formulated early in the fourth century at a time when Christianity had to fight for its dogmatic realizations. For the first three hundred years Christianity did its most effective work in the healing arts as the result of pure religion free from all rigidity of definitions. The early Christians really knew the Truth, hence there was no need of quarreling about definitions and dogma concerning the Truth. When you understand the Truth, you do not quarrel about it. "You shall know the truth and the truth (itself) shall make you free." Rationalizations, creeds, and formulas have no healing power. Truth itself, even unstated, has its own motive power. Truth comes first, thinking about it comes as an afterthought for purposes of explanation and teaching.

Taylor compares what he calls the Christian creed and the pagan creed, and, to say the least, they are amazingly similar. The Nicene Creed, 325 A.D., was an eastern exposition of what is called today the Apostles' Creed. Rome broke away from the Eastern Church which was more mystical.

1. I believe in one God, the Father Almighty, maker of heaven and earth, and of all things visible and invisible.
2. And in Jesus Christ his only son our Lord who was conceived by the Holy Spirit.
3. Born of the Virgin Mary.

4. Suffered under Pontius Pilate.

5. Was crucified.

6. Dead and buried.

7. He descended into hell.

8. The third day he arose again from the dead.

9. He ascended into heaven.

10. And sitteth at the right hand of God, the Father Almighty.

11. From whence he shall come to judge the quick and the dead.

12. I believe in the Holy Ghost, the communion of saints, and the forgiveness of sins.

The simplest way to look at this is to realize that you are Jesus Christ when you begin to practice the Presence of God. Jesus is your illumined reason or intellect. Christ means the Presence of God in your unconscious depths. When you are using your conscious and subconscious mind harmoniously, you are Jesus Christ in action. Your conscious and subconscious mind are projections of the I AM or God within you. The word *son* means expression—you are the son or expression. New Thought stresses the distinction between Jesus (illumined reason) and Christ (subjective self). *I and the Father* means one integrated identification, climaxed by the statement "Who has seen me has seen the Father." The Holy

Ghost or Holy Spirit proceedeth from the Father and the Son. Whatever moves you emotionally is your spirit—your God.

God is first person (spirit).

Son is second person (mental conception, idea, picture, desire).

Holy Spirit is third person (movement of the spirit relative to your desire and your oneness with it).

The hidden symbolism of the Virgin Birth (Jesus' birth) and the Immaculate Conception (Mary's birth) are as follows:

Anna, mother of Mary, means consciousness of love, free from sense of separation from God (*original sin*—psychological separation from God). We, ourselves, embody these phases of consciousness. Anna, Mary, and Jesus are states of consciousness. The Jesus state of consciousness is born of virgin consciousness—untainted by the world. *Suffered under Pontius Pilate* means that your reason and intellect, the governor of your world, attacks your new conception (Jesus) which would save you, i.e., your desire. The unillumined conscious mind seeks to control, limit, and brow-beat the subjective self.

The crucifixion means your new conception is accepted by your mind. The people in your mind (i.e., thoughts and concepts) cry, "Release Barabbas, keep Jesus." All of which means keep that which will save and bless you mentally. Let the negative concept or false beliefs go (Barabbas).

The *cross* means you are always hanging your ideas on the perpendicular beam which is consciousness, infinite, and boundless. Death and birth are really one—disappearance and reappearance on another plane of consciousness.

He descended into hell means your new idea (Jesus) must enter the subjective level through thought and feeling; then the subjective wisdom takes over and carries on without taking thought, and rules now at the right hand of the Father (strong conviction now secured, subjectified). He shall come to judge the quick and the dead. Where are your dead (your ideals, your urges)? Jesus will awaken them. Jesus (the conviction of security) will remove all doubt and discouragement.

To believe in the communion of saints is a process of tuning in to good ideas (saints) and shutting out wrong wave-lengths (false beliefs, fears, doubts).

The Apostles' Creed is really a drama of your own consciousness, and all the characters mentioned are states of consciousness. When you receive holy orders, called *ordination* in New Thought language, you become a minister of a wisdom, an instruction, that transforms your whole life and brings you peace and happiness. You become a minister of Christ. *Christ* means knowledge of God. Christ means the Wisdom, the Truth, and the Beauty of God. You are actually giving to all men wisdom called Christ which, when accepted by them, brings about an interior change. It is truly the science of health, happiness, and peace of mind.

This sacrament is truly received by you when you receive your calling from God; this is called your vocation. This sacrament is a feeling, a mood, a yearning, a longing, and a burning desire to be one with your Father in heaven. It is your desire to be one with all things good. You are under orders to show forth the works of God. You are taught of God; this is the calling of holy orders. You are under orders to bring forth wholeness, peace, beauty, and perfection. You are ordained in the sense that you are under the orders of the Holy One.

A complete copy of an ordination service and what it means is given in one of my books called *Fragrance of God*. As a minister you are to give wisdom to people. Wisdom is more precious than rubies, and all the things you can desire are not to be compared with it. If you have wisdom, you will not need a healing or a bowl of soup or an old suit of clothes. Wisdom is the pearl of great price and the priceless gift of the minister of New Thought; this is why he gives up the lesser for the greater. All his time is devoted to the dispensing of Wisdom or the Light of God to man. It is foolish for a minister of New Thought to dissipate his energy and waste his precious time in various drives, bazaars, blood banks, etc. All the time available should be given to the transfusion of God's Grace and Wisdom into the minds of man. As a minister, your eyes must be dedicated to see the Glories and Beauties of the Deity. Your hands are consecrated to play the sweet melody of God.

Hands are symbolic of direction. With your hands you fashion, mold, and shape. You are now to fashion, mold, and shape all your thoughts, words, and writings to the glory of God. Your feet are to go on errands of God's love and mercy. With your feet you travel from point to point. You teach others how to move psychologically from lack to fulness, from pain to peace, from ignorance to light. Your voice and your words must, from now on, be "like apples of gold" in "pictures of silver." Your words are to be "as a honeycomb," sweet to the ear and pleasant to the bones.

Begin now to feel the Holy Spirit stealing over you. Take the cup and pass it to everyone you see, meet, or visit. "He took the cup and gave thanks, and gave it to them. Drink ye all of it." The *cup* is your heart. The *heart* is the chamber of God's presence. Your heart holds your joy, your love, your goodwill, your life-blood. *Blood* is the life of God; mystically it is the blood of Christ or Wisdom. As you contemplate God's Beauty, and as you feast on God's Love, you find the Love of God welling up in the heart. This cup is sometimes referred to as the Sacred Chalice, the Holy Grail, the vessel that caught Christ's blood on the cross. You perceive, of course, that this language is figurative, allegorical, and mystical. The cup is your mind which is receptive to the truth. Remember always, whatever you meditate on, you invoke the mood or feeling of the idea. In other words, your heart or subjective nature gathers in itself the life which is called the blood of the idea that you are contemplating. Dwell on that which is elevating and dignifying; then you are drinking the blood of Christ, and your cup or heart is becoming full of love and good will.

Drink of that cup and pass it on to the congregation. Let them partake of that cup, that mystic feast. As you continue to contemplate the Glory and Beauty of God, you may enter into a state of ecstasy and experience a union with God which is the moment that lasts forever. Let wisdom be your father, and love your mother. The son from this divine union is health, happiness, peace, and joy. From this moment forward you will listen to no man's voice; neither will you take orders from man or the world of opinion. You will listen to the voice of your father, and your father is God. You are under holy orders—orders of the Holy One.

You are, therefore, to bring forth wholeness, peace, beauty, and perfection. You are also to call it forth in the other person. You are taught of God. Let the Glory of God descend upon you. Claim and feel His healing essence flowing through you. In the silence of your soul you venerate the Deity. God is heard in the silence; Truth is transmitted in the silence; Truth is felt in the silence; for God abides in the silence. "The perfect silence where the lips and heart are still, and we no longer entertain our own imperfect thoughts and vain opinions, but God alone speaks in us, and we wait in singleness of heart that we may know His will, and in the silence of our spirit, that we may do His will and do that only."

Practice this great truth and you have ordained yourself. You are under holy orders and a priest forever according to the order of Melchizedek.

6

The Meaning of Marriage and Divorce

Sacrament of Matrimony

What therefore God hath joined together let no man put asunder; this refers to a spiritual union, a marriage of the heart. In our prayer-life it means this: "When man reaches the absolute conviction that his prayer is answered, this conviction is unshakeable; you are joined to God or your good; the two become one." Those of you who have read my book *Love Is Freedom* which deals at length with marriage, divorce, how to attract your Divine companion, and other articles, are familiar with some of the Truths I am going to elaborate on in this chapter. We must realize that God or the Truth is not present at many marriages.

For example, some months ago I talked to a young lady aged twenty-nine who had been married nine times. She acquired a husband almost every year and after a few weeks or months of married life proceeded to divorce him. The reason for all this was that she was resenting the first husband and had never forgiven him. Therefore, she was attracting men based on her inner state of consciousness.

We don't attract what we want in life, we attract according to our state of consciousness. You can readily see what her state of consciousness was. She was full of resentment, ill will, and bitterness. The subconscious multiplies whatever we meditate on and gives us compound interest; therefore, each of her husbands was progressively worse.

How often is marriage a real sacrament, meaning a spiritual union? How often is it really a legal ceremony against which the parties to the contract begin to chafe in a few weeks? Remember, you marry a state of consciousness. When there is a true, spiritual union between two people ("God hath joined"), there is no divorce for none is wanted. They blend spiritually, mentally, and physically. This is the biblical or spiritual way to pray for a companion, a wife: Close your eyes, be still, think clearly and with interest on the qualities and attributes you admire in a woman, feel that you are now married to such a woman. Know and believe that Infinite Intelligence within you is irresistibly attracting to you the right companion. Infinite

Intelligence takes over when you pray this way and attracts to you a woman who is the image and likeness of the ideal on which you meditated. You will harmonize perfectly and there will be mutual love, freedom, and respect; this is called the "marriage made in heaven" or peace and understanding.*

Many people enter into marriage without ever praying for guidance or right action. Marriage to be real must first be spiritual. There must be a union of two hearts. Many women say to me, "Oh, I want to get married for security" or "I want a home;" this attitude of mind is not correct. Men marry sometimes because the girl is pretty or she has a lot of money or political influence. Such marriages are false because they are not founded on love which is a movement of the heart. The mere fact that they are married in a church does not sanctify the marriage or make it real.

Recently I talked with a woman who was deceived and tricked by her husband. He told her, prior to marriage, that he was a representative for an eastern concern, that he was single, that he belonged to her church organization, etc.—all lies. It turned out that he was an ex-convict, a wife-beater, and was living with another woman when he married her. She had advanced him some money which is what he married

---

* See *Love Is Freedom*

her for. She thought it was a sin to get a divorce; yet she longed for freedom and peace of mind. I explained to her she was not really married at all, that such a marriage was simply a sham, a mockery, and that she was living a lie. She proceeded to get a divorce immediately and dissolved this fraudulent marriage.

Marriage is an accord of divine ideals, a harmony, and purity of purpose. Harmony, honesty, love, and integrity must prevail in the minds and hearts of both husband and wife. If there were a needle in your thumb, you would recognize that the needle does not belong in your thumb but in the pin cushion. Likewise, there are cases of hopeless incompatibility where two people do not belong together any more than a fish belongs on land. It is much better to break up a lie than live a lie.

I recall the case of a young girl during the war who got highly intoxicated one evening and found herself with a marriage certificate next morning. She had married a native of one of the islands. She was shocked beyond words and had to get psychiatric treatment. The answer, of course, was to dissolve the marriage immediately.

Marriage is not a permit by the state for abuse, cruelty, or torture. Marriage is a union of two souls seeking their way to the heart of reality. Each is married to God or good and they see the Christ or Presence of God in each other. The Bible says, "Whosoever shall put away his wife, except it be for fornication, and shall marry another, committeth adultery: and whoso marrieth her which is put away doth commit adultery." MATTHEW 19:9. The word *adultery* means to unite with negative and false concepts of any kind. We are always performing mental marriage acts. Psychologically speaking, man's wife is what he is conscious of being, what he feels as true of himself—his inner conviction or estimate of himself. From this concept or belief about himself, children, such as health, conditions, experiences, and events are born or expressed.

I performed a marriage ceremony for a wonderful young couple in the Middle West one time. In about a month's time they separated and the wife returned to her parents' home. What had happened to their romance? In talking to the young man I found he was practicing adultery or fornication all day long. Adultery means idolatry or worship of false Gods; i.e., giving attention to negative concepts in the mind, forsaking the worship of the one spiritual power within which is the only cause and only power. The young man said to me, "Every day I kept thinking that she would run around with other men. I was jealous of her. I did not trust her. I began to imagine that she was with former boy friends and I was full of fear that I would lose her." He was fornicating in the sense that he was uniting with evil in his mind. The word *fornicate* means to mentally engage or go along with destructive thoughts and negative imagery. (Job says, "What I fear most has come upon me.") The young man was imagining evil about his wife and cohabiting with fear, jealousy, and loss. He had broken his marriage vows wherein he promised to cherish, love, and honor her at all times, and forsaking all others, to remain faithful to her alone.

Before anything happens in our world, it must first take place in the realm of the mind. That is why fornication and adultery really take place first in the mind. This young man's fear was communicated to the subconscious mind of his wife who did not know the laws of mind what he feared and believed actually took place. He saw his belief made manifest; then he blamed his wife. It was done unto him as he believed. When both learned about the workings of their conscious and subconscious mind, they began to pray together; a complete healing of their marital problems followed. "And whoso marrieth her which is put away doth commit adultery."

How often have you put away or failed to remain faithful to your ideal, goal, or objective? When you no longer nourish, feed, and sustain your ideal, but engage in worry and anxiety, you are truly committing adultery and living with another (fear). You have adulterated your ideal by polluting your mind with fear. The young man learned that he should see his wife as she ought to be—radiant, happy, peaceful, and joyous. She also learned to imagine her husband as he ought to be—loyal, faithful, successful, and happy; they lived peacefully afterwards.

What attracted you to your husband? Enumerate the qualities which you admired in him, nourish and sustain these after marriage and cease being a scavenger. Likewise let the husband say to himself, "What were the qualities and characteristics which I admired in my wife and attracted me to her?" Then let him mentally dwell on them and exalt these qualities in his mind. That is seeing the Christ in one another. To practice this will cause your marriage to grow more peaceful through the years. To quote Emerson, "Man is what he thinks all day long." When a man thinks negatively all day long, he eventually becomes ill, morbid, morose, crotchety, and neurotic. This destructive, mental attitude causes him to vent his spleen on his wife, family, and those around him. He is already divorced in his mind for the simple reason that he has separated himself from God or the good. He is cohabiting with evil. He is no longer married to peace, harmony, love, and understanding.

In order for peace and love to prevail in the home it must first prevail in the mind. The Bible is a psychological document; it points out that when man visits the slums in his own mind and keeps company with mental murderers, such as hate, resentment, anger, or ill will, he is cohabiting with evil and therefore guilty of fornication and adultery. In the biblical language he is already divorced; if he keeps up this mental attitude, of course, eventually there will be a separation or divorce on the external plane. The body does nothing except it is acted upon by the mind.

The Bible says, "He that looketh upon a woman, to lust after her, hath already committed adultery with her in his heart." The heart is the seat of the emotions, the feeling nature, the subjective self. Here you are told adultery is of the heart or the mind. The body moves as it is moved upon. Quimby pointed out that the body acts as it is acted upon. When we cleanse our mind, our body will be clean. When our mind is in tune with God, all our actions will be Godlike and noble. Problems in marriage are solved in the same way as any other difficulties—through prayer. Each should see the other radiant, peaceful, happy, and joyous. The wife, for example, in a meditative state imagines her husband is telling her how wonderful and kind she is and how happy he is with her. If she is faithful to this treatment, he will be transformed and peace will be restored.

We must remember that because a man and a woman have a marriage certificate and live in a home, it does not follow that that is a real home. Perhaps it is a place of discord and hate. When a child is present and the parents do not know the law of life, it is better to break up such a union than have the mood of hate stifle the mind of the child. Many times a child's life and mind are dwarfed by the mood of the parents which result in neurosis, crime, etc. It is far better for a boy to live with one parent who loves him than to live with two who hate each other and fight all the time.

The question frequently arises, "Should I get a divorce?" This is an individual problem. It cannot be generalized. In some cases divorce is not the solution any more than marriage is the solution for a lonely man. Divorce may be right for one person and wrong for another. A divorced woman may be far more noble and Godlike than many of her sisters who are living a lie rather than face the truth. In many instances marriage is a sham and a farce. The usual excuses and alibis to cover up are that it would be bad for John's business, or the neighbors might talk, or it is bad politics, etc.; this, of course, is making a mockery of marriage.

The way of prayer will heal the hurts and wounds of married life. If one of the parties gets angry, resentful, or peeved, the thing to do is to immediately heal it by harmonious thinking plus the mood of love and good will. Chop the head off every angry, morbid, critical thought. Cremate them and burn them up with the fire of Divine love. Let husband and wife do this regularly, and the marriage will grow in beauty and love as the years roll by. When the husband or wife engages the mind with evil or destructive thoughts toward the partner, he has deserted God and is an adulterer and fornicator. If he keeps this up, he will become morbid, morose, and hateful. The end result will be either separation, divorce, or annulment of the marriage ties.

I had a rather strange interview one time in Texas. A woman and man came to see me in the hotel in Dallas. They said they had quarrelled over a piece of property a few years previously. They were very angry toward one another and each sued for divorce. They were divorced after about a year in another state. Each had remarried, and they said it was a great mistake. They married on what they called the rebound. They said, "We love each other—what shall we do?" I told them to dissolve the sham and farce of the present marriage and go back to each other, which they did. "Blessed are the meek." They were meek in the sense that they were teachable; they were humble, admitting their mistake of foolish pride, and desire to get even with each other. Divine love led them to each other in the first place. Love heals, restores, opens prison doors, and solves all problems.

Occasionally a woman says to me, "I'm in love with a man but I can't marry him because he is a Jew, a Catholic, or he is not in Truth." This, of course, is absurd. Love knows no creed or religion. Love transcends all these things and knows nothing about the various religions. Love is of God. Let love rule and guide your married life, and the peace of God will reign supreme in that home.

I was asked a few hours ago over the telephone if a father could, by mental means, break up or cause the dissolution of a marriage. It seems the young lady in question married a Catholic and they are deeply in love. Her father, she says, hates Catholics and he belongs to another church. The father tells his daughter that he can, by mental means, get his daughter back. You have seen by now that the girl is afraid of malpractice. I explained to her that her father has no power whatsoever, no more so than an old rabbit's foot or a stone in the field. She began to realize that the only power was in her own thought and consciousness. She began to pray that God's Love unite them and that His Love surround and enfold them. She affirmed that the Grace, the Beauty and the Love of God governed their lives and ruled their hearts.

She knew nothing could come between her and the man she loved. The only power to govern, control, and direct her marriage was her love and devotion to Truth. The sequel to this was that her father's hate was melted in the sunshine of her love.

To maintain a happy married life, pray together and you will stay together. The contemplation of divine ideals, the study of the mysteries of life, a common purpose, plan, and personal freedom bring about that mystic marriage, the wedded bliss, that holy union in which the two should become one. Remain wedded to God and all your ways shall be ways of pleasantness and all your paths shall be paths of peace.

7

Methods of Healing

Extreme Unction

You have been reading about familiar words used in an unfamiliar sense. You read in the Bible that Moses admonished the children of Israel, "Never leave any vessel uncovered." You must learn to keep your conviction as a cover. Keep your illumined conscious mind as a cover over your subconscious mind, or any old opinion or idle belief will come floating in and take over the powers of the subconscious.

Religion comes from *religio* and means "to bind back to." We should be bound to God; but usually we are bound to false gods—to our troubles—beliefs—fears, etc. When you give a spiritual treatment to another, you must keep a cover on your mind, meaning that you reject completely that sickness has any power, and that you speak with authority knowing that God and His Presence are now reflected mentally and physically in the other. As you continue in this conviction results will follow. Do not wander away mentally. Try to keep one-pointed. Religion is essentially the process of making the ideal concept real in form and substance.

The fall of man is the spiritual self forgetting its majesty and glory by putting on the garment of materiality. The only way back to the Father's House is by means of a spiritual rebirth by various stages indicated in the various sacraments—Baptism, Eucharist, Confirmation, Penance, Holy Orders, Matrimony, and Extreme Unction. This whole process in religious terminology is called redemption. We must not lose the beauty and spiritual significance of this process in a maze of ritual, ceremony, and liturgy. A sacrament is a sacred covenant or agreement between the conscious and subconscious mind. When the two agree, you are at peace; this is God in action in your life. The sacraments teach you that man's mission is to reveal the hereness, nowness, and isness of God. Man is an expression of God. When man is really baptized and confirmed, he is married to the Eternal Verities and all mysteries begin to unfold in him. Cease beating about the bush. It is not talking, reading, or thinking about the Truth that does it, but what you believe in your heart that is made manifest. We demonstrate according to the level of our belief.

Every sacrament is an act of union with the Divine resulting in a deeper experience of a downpour of grace. A sacrament is the act of finding or calling forth from the depths of yourself the mood, the feeling fit for your beloved desire.

All the sacraments are dealing with the psychological marriage of the male (idea, desire) with the female—a receptivity of the mind, a conception in which you lose yourself or fall in love—"lose your head." The head is your idea or desire lost or deposited in the subjective mind.

In the sacrament of extreme unction—all openings of the body through which sin may enter are bathed and cleansed with the holy oil of spiritual awareness so that man may not see, hear, or feel evil any more. The Church says extreme unction is that sacrament instituted by Jesus in which, by being anointed with holy oil and having special prayers said by the priest or minister, those who are in danger of death from sickness receive the grace of God. The authority for the sacrament is taken from the book of JAMES which says, "Is any sick among you? let him call for the elders of the church; and let them pray over him, anointing him with oil in the name of the Lord: And the prayer of faith shall save the sick, and the Lord shall raise him up; and if he have committed sins, they shall be forgiven him." JAMES 5:14–15. Anointing with oil is a symbolical act referring to the endowment of man's soul with Divine love. To anoint means to make whole, to illumine, to inspire. "Thou hast anointed my head with oil." PSALMS 23:5. Jesus went up the Mount of Olives, the mountain yielding oil. David went up the Mount of Olives. This is a high state of spiritual awareness. Your highest concept of God is the mountain you climb in prayer. It means a high, exalted state of consciousness. Olive trees and olive oil, which is the oil used in extreme unction, signify the healing power of love. Olive oil is symbolical of the Holy Spirit (the feeling of inner oneness with your desire.)

The *dove* returned to Noah in the ark with an olive leaf in her mouth (the certitude of inner knowing). The two witnesses of *Revelation*, eleventh chapter, are the "two olive trees and the two candlesticks standing before the Lord of the earth." These two refer to love and wisdom.

This is how a young girl in our Bible class gave extreme unction to her mother. She received a telegram from her sister in New York saying that her mother was dying from coronary thrombosis—a similar condition to that from which President Eisenhower suffered. This young girl told me that immediately after receiving the telegram she got still and quiet, went within herself, and began to press out the oil of joy, the oil of gladness, and healing. She began to imagine her sister saying to her over the phone, "Mother had a marvelous healing." She began to hear this over and over again prior to sleep. She felt the joy of it all and said she was lost in the joy of the good news. "Therefore God, thy God, hath anointed thee with the oil of gladness." Psalms 45:7. Her mother had a most remarkable healing much to the amazement of all concerned. In Biblical language she anointed her mother with oil in the name of the Lord.

The *oil* is wisdom and love. Her wisdom consisted in knowing that if she would take the idea of perfect health for her mother and induce the mood of it in her own heart, she would immediately call forth the Power of God relative to that idea, bringing a healing to pass in a way which is past finding out. Her love consisted in seeing her mother as she ought to be— radiant, happy, and free. When you love the other person, you love to see him become and express all that he longs to become and express. In loving the other person, you lift him or her up in consciousness, feeling the truth of what you affirm. This is the *oil* with which you anoint (make whole) him. The *name of the Lord* means the naturalness of the state sought. Name means nature. When the young girl appropriated the mood, the feeling of wholeness for her mother, she was asking in the name of the Lord. There being only one mind, what the daughter felt as true in her mind about her mother was resurrected in the mind of the mother three thousand miles away. "He sent his word and healed them."

"Then took Mary a pound of ointment of spikenard, very costly, and anointed the feet of Jesus, and wiped the feet with her hair: and the house was filled with the odour of the ointment," John 12:3. *Spikenard* means faith in God and in His healing power. You can enter into a delightful mood of love and expectancy like the above-mentioned girl. *Jesus* is your desire, the thing that saves. Your desire must be anointed; i.e., as we contemplate the answer and begin to feel it, we get the reaction which satisfies. This is the fragrant state, the happy state, our house (mind) was filled with the odor of ointment (the answered prayer). *Feet* symbolize understanding of the laws of mind, and hair means power. You wipe the feet of Jesus with your hair when you know that the desire which you turn over with faith and confidence to the subjective power within you will be resurrected by the creative law within you in ways you know not of. "For in that she hath poured this ointment on my body, she did it for my burial." Matthew 26:12. The *burial* is the death of the old state of consciousness and the birth of the new. When your ideal is buried in the subconscious, there takes place the dissolution or death of the old state and the resurrection of the new man.

The odor of the ointment or holy oil is a symbol of bliss, of joy. "An odour of a sweet smell, a sacrifice acceptable, well-pleasing to God." PHILIPPIANS 4:18. The sacrifice you offer is that which elevates, dignifies, and blesses you. The only thing you give to God is the grateful heart. Someone said, "Oh, God, who has done so much for us—give us one more thing—a grateful heart." Whenever we meditate on the great truths of a psalm, we are, biblically speaking, offering a sacrifice to God.

I saw a man who was given a few minutes to live receive extreme unction and an hour afterwards have a remarkable recovery, almost an instantaneous healing. The priest sat by his side. On a table near by were two lighted candles, a plate with some crusts of bread to remove the oil from the priest's fingers, some cotton to remove the oil from the anointed eyes, ears, nose, lips, hands, and feet of the sick person. Sometimes the consecrated oil is called "the oil of the sick." Oil, as you know, has soothing qualities, but rubbing oil on the hands, feet, eyes, ears, etc., of a man will neither heal him nor cure him if he is dying from some disease. Obviously, you must look for some other explanation. You will ask why the above mentioned dying man was healed after the ministration of the priest. The answer is simple when you know the working of the subliminal mind in all men, sometimes referred to as the subconscious mind. The prayers of the priest plus the man's faith in the holy oil administered appealed to the cooperation of the subconscious mind of the sick man. In other words a blind faith was generated embracing an utter reliance on the prayers offered.

It is for the same reason that people are healed at Shinto Shrines and the shrine at Lourdes. In all such cases the healing is due to subconscious belief, though it may be attributed by the person healed to Jesus, the Virgin Mary, or holy oil. An ancient prayer said during the anointing of the sick might be of interest: "With this heavenly anointing, he shall find peace within and without; all pain, all sickness of soul and body are gone." This makes a powerful impression on the minds of some people whatever is impressed in the subconscious mind is expressed in the body and environment. The Bible says the apostles "anointed with oil many sick people and healed them." Mark 6:13. We do not take this literally. The girl mentioned in this chapter who prayed for her mother anointed her with oil three thousand miles away in the true meaning of the word.

Before receiving extreme unction, the one who receives it confesses his sins and receives absolution.

When the priest calls upon the Lord, the Holy Virgin, St. Joseph, etc., to uplift the man, all this has a profound effect on the receptive minds of some sick people and oftentimes a healing or recovery follows.

Another interesting case will illustrate what I mean when I say recovery sometimes follows the administration of this sacrament. I knew a man who was a chronic alcoholic, had committed various crimes, and found himself at the end of the rope. His mother had brought him up a devout Catholic; so when he was apparently on his deathbed, he sent the nurse to get a priest. He confessed all his crimes and sins, received absolution and the sacrament of extreme unction which we have already explained. He seemed radiant and happy afterwards. The reason for this was that he now had a deep inner faith and conviction that he was on the right side of God and all was forgiven. He relaxed and was ready for what he termed "Heaven." The nurse and doctor noted a remarkable improvement and the prognosis was made that he would live. In ten days he was whole and perfect. The man is now eighty-two years old and is still very strong and healthy. How did all this come about? The answer is not in the wafer or the oil administered. It was the relaxed attitude, his surrender to God which immediately released his mind and body from the pressures of pain, fear, guilt, and hatred. His body responded in a miraculous manner to the new mental attitude. His inner sense of freedom and peace of mind was the healing agent and nothing else. The mechanism of the healing was not due to the wafer and the oil; the latter was merely a perceptible sign, a practical means of creating concrete his faith in God.

Many people do not understand that extreme unction is the sacrament of the sick, and the word *death* is never mentioned in the prayer. A Catholic who is sick may ask for extreme unction if he thinks his sickness is serious and receive it. The Infinite Healing Presence of God in present everywhere and is in all men and responds to our belief. There is only one process of healing and it is the exercise of faith. "Thy faith hath made thee whole." When a Catholic hears the following prayer at extreme unction, it may well have an effect upon him and kindle the faith necessary to cause the Healing Principle to respond. "Heal, O Redeemer, the infirmities of the sick person, heal his wounds and forgive his sins. Make all the infirmities of his body and soul disappear and by your mercy give him full spiritual and corporal health."

The Bible says, "The prayer of faith will save the sick man and the Lord (the subconscious mind) will raise him up." JAMES 5:15. It is faith that brings the healing, not the ritual, ceremony, oil, or wafer. Faith is just belief in the mind—a thought which you accept as true. A person condemned to death receives the sacrament, viaticum, or holy communion, which sacrament was explained in a previous chapter. He does not receive the sacrament of the sick (extreme unction), for the obvious reason—he is not sick.

The symbolism and spiritual significance of anointing the eyes, ears, etc., is as follows: Your eyes are anointed that you may see the glory and the Truth of God; your ears that you may hear and understand the truth; your nostrils that you may reject all mental food unfit for the house of God; your lips that the words of your mouth and the meditations of your heart may be acceptable to God; your hands that they may mold, fashion, and create according to God's perfect pattern and play the sweet melody of God; the feet that you may always travel in love and on errands of mercy and good will.

We have gone through the seven sacraments representing seven lights or degrees of awareness. Seven is the number of fulness. Seven denotes the sabbath, the stillness, the rest which follows true prayer. Many times you pray about a certain subject until you have a definite feeling that your prayer is answered. There is then no need to pray further; furthermore, there is no desire to do so. You are possessed by an inner certitude and trust. This is called the seventh day or extreme unction—the last step in the healing of the situation or condition.

The first step is: Baptism. Cleansing the mind, knowing that my desire is my savior.

2: Confirmation. Becoming convinced that God—the Spiritual Power within—will bring my desire to pass. I reject completely all negative thoughts by reminding myself that the Spirit within is the only Power.

3: Penance. I change my thought and keep it changed. I quietly focus my thought on my desire, knowing the Almighty Power is responsive to my thought.

4: Eucharist. I mentally feast on the reality of my desire, and as I do, I generate the blood or life of the idea. I make it alive within me; I animate, nourish, and sustain it.

5: Holy Orders. My feeling is the priest which mediates between the invisible and visible state. I continue to dwell on the reality of my desire by imagining and feeling the reality of it. I am now changing to the consciousness of victory and truth.

6: Marriage. My conscious and subconscious mind are now in perfect agreement and there is no argument. I am one emotionally with my desire. There is a psychological marriage and a wave of peace has come over me. God is present now. I rest and relax. The mental creative act is finished.

7: Extreme Unction. I am anointed. I am at peace. I have reached the sabbath—a sense of stillness. I am unmoved, unconcerned. I walk in the assumption that my prayer is answered. There is no effort or work on my part. I have reached the sabbath, the seventh hour, and it was the seventh hour He was healed.

About the Author

A native of Ireland who resettled in America, Joseph Murphy, Ph.D., D.D. (1898–1981) was a prolific and widely admired New Thought minister and writer, best known for his metaphysical classic, *The Power of Your Subconscious Mind*, an international bestseller since it first appeared on the self-help scene in 1963. A popular speaker, Murphy lectured on both American coasts and in Europe, Asia, and South Africa. His many books and pamphlets on the auto-suggestive and metaphysical faculties of the human mind have entered multiple editions—some of the most poignant of which appear in this volume. Murphy is considered one of the pioneering voices of affirmative-thinking philosophy.

Printed in the USA
CPSIA information can be obtained
at www.ICGtesting.com
JSHW012033140824
68134JS00033B/3034